The VICTORY COOKBOOK

First published in the U.K. in 1995
by Hamlyn
an imprint of Octopus Publishing Group Limited
2-4 Heron Quays, London E14 4JP

Reprinted in 2000

ISBN 0 600 60254 0

A CIP catalogue record for this book is available from the British Library.

Printed in China

Note: Both imperial and metric measurements have been given in all recipes. Use one set of measurements only and not a mixture of both.

the VICTORY COOKBOOK

Marguerite Patten O.B.E.

HAMLYN

Keep
Smi
ling
IT'S V-E DAY!
GERMANY SURRENDERS
GERMANY SURRENDERS
GERMANY

contents

FOREWORD

I am sure everyone will understand the feelings of the British people, and indeed people throughout the world, when the Second World War ended.

The official announcement of Victory in Europe came in a broadcast by the Prime Minister, Winston Churchill, who said *'The German War is at an end. Evil-doers are prostrate before us'.*

King George VI wrote in his diary, *'The Day we have been longing for has arrived at last and we can look back with thankfulness to God that our tribulation is over.'*

May 8 was Victory Day (VE Day) in Europe but the war was not yet completely over. The end came on August 14 - VJ Day - when the Japanese surrendered.

May 8 1945 was a night of celebrations indeed. Londoners, and anyone who could get to London, and within sight of Buckingham Palace, came there. My sister and I joined these crowds. We cheered and cheered until we were hoarse, at the sight of the King and Queen, with Princess Elizabeth, now our Queen, and her sister Margaret, together with Winston Churchill, on the balcony of the Palace.

Total strangers embraced each other, there was laughter, dancing and great thankfulness. At last we could get to bed without fear of being wakened by air-raids. The men and women in the forces in Europe would be returning. Similar celebrations took places in cities, towns and villages throughout Britain and in many countries of the world.

Anyone who had family or friends concerned with the war in Japan still had the worry about their safety; but those worries ended in August on VJ Day and there were wholehearted rejoicings again. As members of the forces and prisoners of war returned home everyone celebrated once again. During the war, we in Britain had become a very united and caring community. You could be certain that if one family in a street was awaiting news of a returning serviceman, or woman, other people living around them would share their worries and their joy, when that person was finally safely home.

The festivities, in one form or another, went on for a long time and many events took place throughout Britain. In this book I have recorded some of these .

I was in charge of the Ministry of Food Bureau at Harrods and I well remember being asked by people to plan celebration meals for weeks during 1945. Generally my first question on being asked to give suggestions for the menu was 'what food have you got?' for that determined the kind of party you would be able to give. We had won the war but it did not change the fact that food was still rationed, and likely to be for some time to come. Of course in 1945 we had no idea that it would be 1954 before rationing finally ended.

There were the family celebrations. The food might have to be simple, and still wartime fare, but the occasions were wonderful. Neighbourhoods also held large parties which, in many cases, took place in the streets, for these were the only places large enough to hold all the people who attended, many halls having been bombed. 1945 seemed to be a lucky year for weather and I do not recall street parties being spoiled by rain. Among the street parties were many for children or for the elderly, who had endured so much.

While details of Victory celebrations fill much of this book, the last chapter covers the period from 1945 to the end of rationing in 1954.

I hope you will enjoy reading,and trying out as many as possible of the recipes in this book and that they will make you feel you are joining with the British and their Allies from all over the world who celebrated 50 years ago - on VE and VJ days in 1945.

Marguerite Patten

INTRODUCTION

The immediate period before Victory was certainly not a peaceful one. Fighting was intense both in Europe and in the Far East.

The Home Front, as we at home were known in Britain, continued to cope with the perils of flying bombs and rockets together with more personal worries. The problem of rationing had become a familiar one and people were managing well. We also became like squirrels, hoarding summer foods for the winter.

Seasonal fruits and tomatoes were bottled. Onions were a problem, too, for shipping space was far too valuable to import onions. so people dried as many as possible to give flavour to winter dishes.

The Women's Institutes and other organisations achieved wonderfully high standards when preserving fruits. They made jam, on behalf of the Ministry of Food and to the Ministry's specifications, to form part of the rations. The jars of bottled fruit put on show by them and those of us in the Food Advice Division of the Ministry were often artistically perfect - every piece of rhubarb would be the same length and beautifully packed. You would see jars of apple rings, with blackberries nestling in the centre of each apple ring.

Dig for Victory was a message observed by a very large percentage of the public. You could see vegetables growing among the roses and other plants in gardens, and some people even dug up all their flowers to plant a variety of vegetables and fruits instead.

In the country it was taken for granted that people would keep chickens, but many town dwellers decided to keep them, too, to give them fresh eggs and provide a chicken to cook from time to time. Some of my friends had invested in poultry, and a few had rabbits too. Many of the latter were never eaten, for they became family pets and no-one could bear to kill them.

THE MINISTRY OF FOOD

The Ministry controlled the distribution of food during the war, and afterwards, and was responsible for giving out information on food rationing, and the wise use of all foods. The recipes and Food Facts leaflets published by the Ministry of Food enabled people to make the best use of the rations available and augment them with unrationed foods, such as potatoes, flour, oatmeal and seasonal vegetables. Much of the advice was given in a light-hearted manner. In addition to recipes and suggestions for new ways of incorporating more potatoes into the daily diet, for instance, the value of the vegetable was extolled by the symbol 'Potato Pete'. Children became interested in Potato Pete's friendly figure and advice and were more inclined to eat, and enjoy, potato dishes.

A Food Advice Division was established within the Ministry of Food to help ensure that the public kept fit on the rations and enjoyed the dishes they could make with the food available.

The headquarters staff in London were responsible for nutritional information and the recipes published by the Ministry. Throughout Britain Food Advice Centres were established, staffed by home economists, of whom I was one. We gave demonstrations in the Centres, and in market squares, hospital out-patient departments, works' canteens, large stores or any place where we could come into contact with people, for it was essential that everybody knew about the rations and any additional foods to which they were entitled.

In April 1940 Lord Woolton became Minister of Food and his name soon became very well-known. Although a recipe for the famous Woolton Pie, named after him, has already been given in my book on wartime cooking, We'll Eat Again, I have repeated it for, since that book was published, I have found that there are several versions, all of which are interesting.

FOOD RATIONING

Not all basic foods were placed on the ration at one time; foods were introduced gradually:

January 1940 - *rationing introduced. The foods placed on ration were: bacon, ham, sugar and butter.*

March 1940 - *meat became a rationed food.*

July 1940 - *tea, margarine, cooking fat and cheese made part of the ration.*

March 1941 - *jam, marmalade, treacle and syrup all put on ration.*

June 1941 - *distribution of eggs controlled.*

November 1941 -*distribution of milk controlled.*

July 1942 - *sweets put on ration.*

WELFARE FOODS

The Vitamin Welfare Scheme was introduced in December 1941. Small children and expectant mothers received cod liver oil and concentrated orange juice (from America). These played a major part in ensuring that children grew up strong and healthy. Expectant and nursing mothers and small children were entitled to extra milk rations, too, as were certain invalids.

WHAT WERE THE RATIONS?

These were the basic rations for one person per week. The ration book had coupons, covering the different ration foods, which were removed as the food was purchased. The basic rations varied slightly from time to time, as more or less of a certain food was available, but on the whole they were as follows:

BACON / HAM *4 oz (100 g) of either bacon or ham.*

MEAT *to the value of 1s 2d (6p in today's money). Sausages were not rationed but often difficult to obtain. Offal was originally not rationed but when supplies of meat were difficult it formed part of the ration. Canned corned beef and products like Spam generally formed part of the points system.*

BUTTER *2 oz (50 g).*

CHEESE *2 oz (50 g). Sometimes this rose to 4 oz (100 g) and very occasionally to 8 oz (225 g). Vegetarians had extra cheese, for they surrendered their meat coupons.*

MARGARINE *4 oz (100 g).*

COOKING FAT *4 oz (100 g) but quite often this dropped to 2 oz (50 g). Dripping, sometimes mentioned in recipes, was scrapings from every frying pan or pot to obtain every spoonful of dripping. This was not available on rations.*

MILK *3 pints (1.8 litres), often dropping to 2 pints (1.2 litres). National Dried Milk (known as Household milk), which became available after December 1941, was a tin per 4 weeks.*

SUGAR *8 oz (225 g), which had to be used for cooking and jam-making too. When there were adequate supplies in the country the Ministry would release a little more for jam-making; this was available on the sugar coupon.*

PRESERVES *1 lb (450 g) very 2 months, so it was very important to supplement this (Jam, marmalade, with home-made preserves, golden syrup or treacle).*

EGGS *1 shell egg a week, if available, but frequently dropping to 1 shell egg every 2 weeks. From June 1942 dried eggs were available and the ration was a packet (containing the equivalent of 12 eggs) each 4 weeks.*

TEA *2 oz (50 g) per week. In December 1944 an extra tea allowance was introduced for 70-year-olds and over.*

SWEETS *12 oz (350 g) every 4 weeks.*

THE POINTS SYSTEM

Each person was allowed 16 points per month and one had to choose how to use these points; for example, they allowed you to buy:

1 can of meat or fish or

2 lb (900 g) dried fruit or

8 lb (3.6 kg) split peas or similar pulses.

Canned fruit was also available on points.

RATION BOOKS FOR ALL

TO ADD TO THE RATIONS

National Dried Milk was a great help in augmenting the fresh milk ration. The flavour was not the same as fresh milk so it was mostly used in cooking. It was not the same as the milk powders produced to feed babies.

At first, we disliked dried egg intensely, mainly because we did not appreciate just how carefully one should reconstitute it. Quite quickly, though, we found that if you took just one absolutely level tablespoon of dried egg powder and carefully blended it with 2 tablespoons of water you had a very good product.

There were many recipes in which you could add the dried egg powder to the flour, or other ingredients, and not reconstitute it. In this case, you needed to add the 2 tablespoons of water to the rest of the liquid in the dish. As we got used to dried egg we found that most egg dishes could be made with it, including omelettes, scrambled eggs, Yorkshire Pudding batters, cakes of all kinds, even sponges and, surprisingly, a soufflé!

EATING AWAY FROM HOME

By the end of 1944 it was estimated that about 9% of all food in Britain was consumed outside the home. There were approximately 147,000 catering establishments, serving 23,000,000 daily meals. They played an important part in supplementing the rations, as no ration cards or coupons had to be given up.

2000 British Restaurants were opened in towns and cities in Britain. The food was relatively inexpensive and comparable to good school dinners.

It was compulsory for factories to provide canteens. By the end of 1944 there were 30,500 in existence.

School meals were an essential part of catering and for many children were a real treat. By February 1945 1,850,000 school meals were served each day.

In addition to these places, restaurants of all kind were open. It was illegal to charge more than 5s 0d (25p) per meal, though large and expensive establishments were allowed to make cover charges.

Helping hands...

EXTRA BENEFITS

Some people were entitled to additional food. People doing extra heavy work and munition workers were allowed extra meat. Agricultural workers, who could not benefit from canteen facilities, were allowed an extra cheese ration

EMERGENCY FEEDING

After bomb attacks, gas, electricity and water facilities were often out of action and homeless people had to be sheltered and fed. Mobile kitchens were rushed to bombed areas and W.V.S. and A.R.P. workers were there to give sympathy and provide plentiful cups of hot tea, coffee and food. Queen's Messenger Convoys were able to move around the area quickly to give help.

DEALING WITH SHORTAGES

FOOD Because food was so important, during and after the war, it was an offence to waste any. In fact, if people were discovered wasting food, legal proceedings could be taken against them.

PAPER Paper was very scarce and we saved all wrappings from any fat and used it to cover food, especially during cooking in the oven. Greaseproof bags were cut up to line cake tins.

FUEL Saving fuel was essential, so hay-box cookery became important.. A hay-box could be made from a large square biscuit tin or box with a well-fitting lid. Pads were made from hay, enclosed in cloth and fitted inside the base, the sides and lid of the container. Stews and soups were partially cooked in the oven, then placed inside the hay-box where they continued cooking, without using fuel.

Large vacuum flasks were often used in the same way to tenderize prunes or other dried fruit. The fruit would be well-soaked, half-cooked, then transferred to the flask to complete the cooking process.

The flasks were also used to keep soup hot; often left-over tea was strained from the teapot into a vacuum flask to be served later, so saving precious tea. It would be ready for people working late on ARP duties to take with them.

Steamers were used a great deal, for several kinds of food could be cooked over one pan of boiling water.

MANAGING ON THE RATIONS

Today the medical profession and nutritionists claim that we were healthier in the days of rationing than we are today, when there is such an abundance of food available. So what kept us so healthy?

Before mentioning food I feel I must stress that our emotions at the time played a great part in keeping us going. We people at home could not let the forces down, we had to play our part too. Most people worked very long hours in various jobs and also took part in voluntary activities in the ARP (Air Raid Precaution Services) and the WVS (Women's Voluntary Services) who were always there to help in times of

We all liked Mrs. Parker, in the city, until we heard she wasted crusts (a pity!).

emergency. Everyone in the Kitchen Front felt it was their duty to keep healthy to carry on.

Undoubtedly, our good health came from well-balanced meals, although probably few people realised they were good at the time, they seemed so horribly monotonous and catering was an endless problem.

In addition to the basic rations our meals were based on these unrationed foods:

BREAD (and flour-based foods). The National bread and flour were certainly not as light as we would wish and the flour did make baking more difficult (allied to the lack of fat, sugar and eggs for baking). The Ministry

also introduced wholemeal bread and flour (generally known as wheatmeal), which had more flavour than the National white bread and flour. Oatmeal was also strongly recommended as part of a healthy diet, and was used in bread and biscuit recipes.

FISH - usually available in fairly small quantities only, unless you lived by the sea and were fortunate enough to have freshly caught fish.

VEGETABLES - this is where we augmented the small rations of meat, cheese and eggs. You may be surprised at the very generous amount of vegetables included in recipes in this book. Most people ate that amount to satisfy their appetites; even if they were not great vegetable lovers. Vegetables were eaten raw in salads and cooked, too. I am sure it was during the war years that the British learned how to cook vegetables correctly, so they retained flavour, colour and texture plus valuable mineral salts and vitamins.

FRUIT - which was in limited supply, particularly in wintertime. Citrus fruits (except for very rare, and small, amounts of fresh oranges which were only sold on children's ration books) were unknown, like other fruits that used to be imported. Adults had to get their intake of vitamins from raw vegetables; children from the excellent welfare foods supplied.

There were also limited supplies of canned fish and meat available on the points system, described on page 8, and small amounts of sausages, liver and other offal for which you generally had to form a queue at the butcher's shop.

Wartime food was not exciting, but we were not under-fed, nor were we hungry, as were people in many countries in Europe and other parts of the world. While rationing made it possible for everyone to be adequately fed, there is no doubt that we would all have been very unhappy indeed had we known in 1945 that rationing was to continue for several years to come - and would not finally come to an end until after the Coronation of our present Queen..

Although Victory Days celebrations and the food eaten then take up much of this book, I felt the British people deserved a tribute to their victory in coping with those years of rationing and food shortages. Therefore, the last chapter in this book covers the period from 1945 to the end of rationing in 1954, and includes the kind of recipes we used when various foods, such as oranges and other citrus fruits, bananas, extra kinds of cheese and many other ingredients gradually became available to use free of rationing again.

FAMILY CELEBRATIONS

Practically every household throughout Britain celebrated the Victory Days. The rations did not permit magnificent spreads of food but family cooks would certainly do their best to make everyday dishes look as festive as possible. Often, families were joined by overseas servicemen, especially Americans, at the celebrations.

The fact that VE Day and VJ Day came during the late spring and the summer was a great help, for it was easier to cater in summertime when there were homegrown tomatoes, lettuce, cucumber and other salad ingredients and an appreciable amount of summer fruits.

In this chapter I have concentrated chiefly on dishes for main meals, including the kind of soups, salads, fish, meat and vegetable dishes and the puddings that could have appeared on tables in all parts of the country on those two wonderfully happy days.

SOUPS

A meal during the years of rationing often included a soup and, for Victory celebrations, they would be an obvious choice as the first course of a celebration meal.

The recipes here give a variety of flavours and include soups suitable for a chilly or a beautifully hot day. They make good use of the variety of vegetables that are available during the various months of the year. A well-flavoured soup is a good start to any meal and helps to satisfy the appetite of hungry people.

Onion Soup

Preparation time: 15 minutes

Cooking time: 40 minutes

Quantity: 4 helpings

When there are onions available do make this soup. If you have no onions in wintertime then try the recipe using leeks instead.

1 lb (450 g) onions, thinly sliced
1 oz (25 g) margarine or cooking fat or dripping
1½ pints (900 ml) beef or vegetable stock or water
little yeast extract
salt and pepper
4 small slices bread
1 oz (25 g) cheese, grated

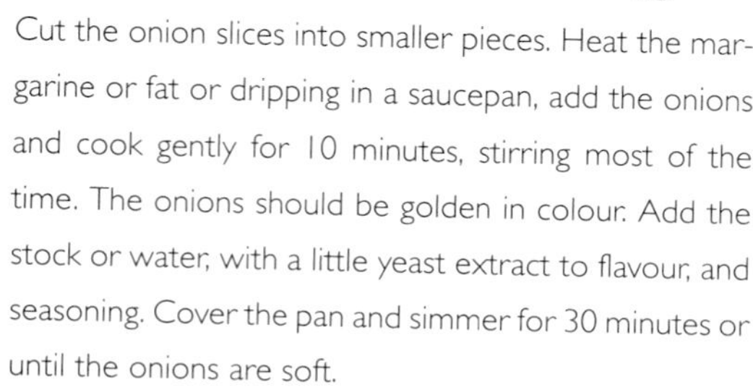

Cut the onion slices into smaller pieces. Heat the margarine or fat or dripping in a saucepan, add the onions and cook gently for 10 minutes, stirring most of the time. The onions should be golden in colour. Add the stock or water, with a little yeast extract to flavour, and seasoning. Cover the pan and simmer for 30 minutes or until the onions are soft.

Toast the bread, ladle the soup into soup plates or bowls, top with the toast and cheese and serve.

Leek and Potato Soup

Preparation time: 20 minutes

Cooking time: 25 minutes

Quantity: 4 helpings

2 pints (1.2 litres) vegetable stock or water
4 medium leeks, thinly sliced
12 oz (350 g) potatoes, cut into ½ inch (1 cm) dice
salt and pepper
2 tablespoons chopped parsley
little cayenne pepper (optional)
1 oz (25 g) margarine (optional)

Bring the stock or water to the boil, add the leeks and potatoes and seasoning. Cover the pan and simmer for 25 minutes or until the vegetables are tender. Do not over-cook the soup or the leeks will lose colour.

Add the parsley, cayenne pepper and margarine, if you can spare this, at the end of the cooking time. The margarine is not essential but does improve the taste.

Summer Beetroot Soup

Preparation time: 15 minutes

Cooking time: 10 minutes

Quantity: 4 helpings

Serve this excellent summertime soup hot or cold.

1 pint (600 ml) water
4 small or 2 medium cooked beetroot, skinned and coarsely grated
4 medium tomatoes, skinned and finely diced
4 tablespoons chopped spring onions
2 tablespoons chopped parsley
salt and pepper

Bring the water to the boil, add the ingredients and cook gently for 10 minutes. Serve hot or allow the soup to become cold and well-chilled then serve.

Variation: Use the same recipe in wintertime but substitute a large finely chopped onion for the spring onions. Simmer this in the water for 10-15 minutes then add the beetroot and about 8 oz (225 g) bottled tomato purée and continue as in the recipe above. Omit the fresh tomatoes.

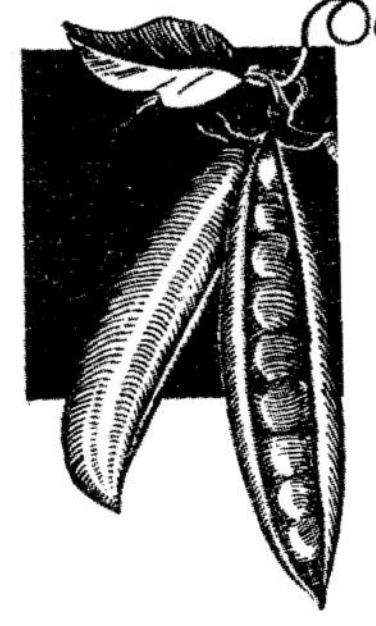

Green Pea Soup

Preparation time: 25 minutes

Cooking time: 30-35 minutes

Quantity: 4-6 helpings

When you have tender young peas do not waste the pods: use them to make a delicious soup.

1½ lb (675 g) peas in pods
1 oz (25 g) margarine
2 small onions, chopped
1¼ pints (750 ml) water
1 sprig mint
salt and pepper
1 teaspoon sugar
To garnish:
chopped mint
chopped chives or parsley

Wash the peas, do not remove the peas from the pods but trim away any stalks and discard any damaged pods, using the peas from them. Heat the margarine in a pan, add the onions and cook gently for 5 minutes, so they do not become brown. Pour the water into the saucepan, bring to the boil, add the pea pods, mint, salt and pepper and sugar. Cook steadily for 20-25 minutes, or until the pods are very tender.

Rub the soup through a sieve, return to the saucepan, taste and add any extra seasoning required, then reheat for 5 minutes. Top with the freshly chopped herb garnish and serve.

Variations: When the peas are older, use 12 oz (350 g) peas, without pods, and prepare the soup as above.

Creamy Pea Soup: use 1 pint (600 ml) water and add ¼ pint (150 ml) milk or top of the milk or unsweetened evaporated milk after the peas have been sieved and reheat.

Lentil Soup

Preparation time: 25 minutes

Cooking time: 1 hour

Quantity: 4-6 helpings

8 oz (225 g) split lentils
2 medium onions, finely chopped
2 medium carrots, finely diced
1-2 bacon rashers, derinded and chopped
1½ pints (900 ml) water
1 tablespoon chopped parsley
1 teaspoon chopped fresh thyme or ½ teaspoon dried thyme
salt and pepper

Wash the lentils. If possible, soak them in cold water to cover for several hours, to reduce the cooking time. Strain the lentils and discard the soaking water. Put the lentils into a saucepan with the vegetables and bacon, including the rinds, for these add flavour. Add the water and herbs; season the soup lightly. Cover the pan and simmer for 1 hour. Remove the bacon rinds, taste the soup and add more seasoning, if required, then serve.

Variations: Creamy Lentil Soup: use 1 pint (600 ml) water. Make a thin White Sauce with ½ oz (15 g) margarine, ½ oz (15 g) flour and ½ pint (300 ml) milk, blend into the soup just before serving and heat briefly.

Leek and Lentil Soup: use 4 oz (100 g) lentils and 4 small sliced leeks. Add the leeks after the soup has been simmering 30 minutes. Omit bacon, if you wish.

Note. To save fuel, cook the soup in a covered casserole in the oven when in use. It takes about 1½ hours in a preheated oven, 160°C (325°F), Gas Mark 3.

A salad a day

The seasonal salads here come from a Ministry of Food leaflet. Equivalents of the cup measures included in the recipes are: teacup is equivalent to ¼ pint (150ml) and a breakfast cup to ½ pint (300 ml).

'We used to think of a salad as just a pleasant little addition to cold meat,' says the Ministry of Food leaflet. 'Now that we have found out more about foods we have discovered how rich in value salads are. There is hardly a root or green vegetable that does not deserve a place in a salad. Use them raw whenever you can.

When making salads, touch the plants as little as possible. Keep in a cold place until needed; a saucepan with a well-fitting lid is excellent if placed on a cool floor.

Just before serving, wash carefully, shake off the water gently and dry the plants in a clean cloth or wire salad basket. Keep outside tough leaves for soups.

VINAIGRETTE DRESSING

Mix together 2 tablespoons salad oil, 1 tablespoon good quality vinegar, salt and pepper to taste, a little mustard and a pinch of sugar (optional). If liked, add chopped fresh herbs, such as parsley or thyme (or a pinch of dried herbs). Instead of herbs, try 1 or 2 crushed garlic cloves.

SPRING SALADS

(1) Make a thick bed of chopped raw cabbage heart in your bowl. In the centre pile a grated raw white turnip. Round this centre pile arrange smaller piles of grated raw carrot and grated raw beetroot (using a teacup of each). Decorate with radishes and parsley.

(2) Shred 8 oz (225 g) young turnip tops. Mix with 1 breakfastcup of diced cooked potatoes and 1 breakfastcup of diced cooked beetroot. Put into a bowl and decorate the top with 1 large grated carrot and sprigs of watercress and dandelion leaves.

(3) Young dandelion leaves make a delightful salad. Cut off the roots, wash the clusters of leaves well, dry in a cloth and toss in a Vinaigrette dressing (see box, left). Add a grated raw vegetable - carrot, parsnip or swede - and a few chopped spring onions.

SUMMER SALADS

(1) Line a bowl with crisp lettuce leaves. Mix together 1 breakfastcup each of cooked peas, cooked diced potatoes and cooked diced carrots. Pile the mixture into the bowl and serve with mint sauce.

(2) Line a bowl with crisp lettuce leaves. Put in a breakfastcup cooked broad beans, a breakfastcup grated raw carrots and a medium-sized cucumber, diced. Decorate with a few nasturtium leaves and parsley.

(3) Mix together a breakfastcup of cooked runner beans cut into 1 inch (2.5 cm) lengths and a breakfastcup cooked diced potatoes and a large lettuce, shredded. Decorate with sliced tomato and a few chopped spring onions, if possible.

AUTUMN SALADS

(1) Break a cauliflower into sprigs and steam them or boil them in a little salted water. When cold, arrange on a bed of lettuce with a breakfastcup of sliced cooked potatoes. Decorate with parsley and a sliced tomato.

(2) Allow 1 small cooked beetroot per person. Hollow out the centre and fill with a mixture of chopped apple

or pear and chopped celery, moistened with mayonnaise. Arrange the beets on a bed of salad greens and surround with little heaps of grated raw carrot, diced cooked potatoes and the beetroot centres, diced.

(3) Wash and dry young celery leaves. Toss them lightly in Vinaigrette dressing (page 16) and serve with diced cooked beetroot or grated raw beetroot.

WINTER SALADS

(1) Make 3 tablespoons Vinaigrette dressing (page 16) in a bowl. Put in 2 teacups grated raw cabbage heart and 1 teacup each diced cooked potatoes, diced raw apples and celery. Turn in the dressing with a wooden spoon. Decorate with watercress.

(2) Mix together 2 teacups grated raw cabbage heart, 2 teacups grated raw carrot and 1 teacup grated raw swede. Decorate with green celery tops and a little grated raw cauliflower.

(3) Line your bowl thickly with watercress, add 8 oz (225 g) chicory, cut into thin strips and mixed with 1 breakfastcup of grated raw beetroot. Serve with Vinaigrette dressing.

Egg Mayonnaise

PREPARATION TIME: 10 MINUTES

COOKING TIME: 10 MINUTES

QUANTITY: 4 HELPINGS

1 reconstituted dried egg or fresh egg
1 tablespoon milk
1 tablespoon salad oil
1 tablespoon vinegar
½-1 teaspoon made mustard
salt and pepper
pinch sugar (optional)

Put all the ingredients in a basin, stand over a saucepan of hot, but not boiling, water and whisk until thick and creamy. Remove from the heat and continue whisking as the mixture cools The mixture will keep in a covered jar in a cool place for several days. If it becomes rather thick, thin it with a little milk.

Spiced Mayonnaise

PREPARATION TIME: 10 MINUTES

COOKING TIME: 10 MINUTES

QUANTITY: 4 HELPINGS

2 reconstituted dried eggs
3 tablespoons salad oil
1-2 teaspoons Worcestershire sauce
1 tablespoon mushroom ketchup
1-2 tablespoons vinegar
½-1 teaspoon made mustard
salt and pepper

Hard-boil the eggs (Cabbage Casserole, page 26). Rub them through a sieve, then add the rest of the ingredients gradually to give a smooth mixture.

Variations: With shell eggs use the yolks only of 2-3 eggs. Use the chopped hard-boiled whites in the salad.

Creamy Egg Mayonnaise: hard-boil 2 reconstituted dried eggs (page 26). Rub through a sieve then gradually blend in 4 tablespoons top of the milk or better still unsweetened evaporated milk, if you can spare this. When smooth, beat in 1 tablespoon vinegar, ½-1 teaspoon made mustard, a little salt and pepper and a good pinch of sugar.

Herb Mayonnaise: To the Creamy Egg Mayonnaise add 1 peeled and crushed garlic clove and 2 tablespoons chopped mixed herbs (parsley, thyme, tarragon etc).

EGGLESS MAYONNAISE

When eggs are not available or in very short supply, try this eggless mayonnaise. Mash one small cooked and skinned potato until very smooth, then add 1 teaspoon made mustard and 2 tablespoons vinegar (or to taste). Very slowly blend in 4 fl oz (125 ml) salad oil. Season with salt and pepper to taste.

FISH DISHES

These are some of the fish dishes that would be served during the period between VE and VJ Days.

Although fish was not rationed it was not available in large quantities and the selection of fish was limited. Many fishermen were serving in the Royal and Merchant navies. Often the fish had taken a long time to come from the coast to fish shops and, therefore, was not as fresh as it should be. This is why strong flavours, such as spices, were often used in fish dishes.

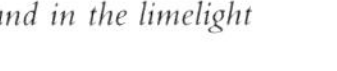

Each time we serve a meal we stand in the limelight

Fish Roast

Preparation time: 10 minutes

Cooking time: 30 minutes

Quantity: 4-6 helpings

This is an excellent way of cooking a large piece of fish, or a whole fish, in the oven. When roasted it has an attractive brown and crisp skin.

2 lb (900 g) cod or fresh haddock, cut in one piece
8 oz (225 g) tomatoes, thickly sliced
salt and pepper
1 oz (25 g) cooking fat or dripping, melted

Remove the fins from the fish and make about 4 shallow cuts across the top of the fish joint. Insert some of the tomato slices in the pockets made in the fish. Season the fish lightly and brush with the melted fat or dripping. Put into a roasting tin.

Preheat the oven to 200°C (400°F), Gas Mark 6 and bake for 30 minutes, basting with the small amount of fat or dripping in the tin once or twice. Add any tomato slices left to the roasting tin about 10 minutes before the end of the cooking time.

Variation: Use finely chopped spring onions in place of the sliced tomatoes.

Swedish Herrings

Preparation time: 15 minutes

Cooking time: 25 minutes

Quantity: 4 helpings

4 herrings, cleaned and filleted
1-2 teaspoons salt
2 tablespoons vinegar
2 tablespoons water
1½ tablespoons sugar
shake pepper
pinch ground cloves
2 tablespoons crisp browned breadcrumbs

Rub the herring fillets with the salt, place in a baking dish, with the fillets slightly overlapping. Mix the vinegar, water, sugar, pepper and cloves together. Spoon over the herrings. Top with the crumbs.

Preheat the oven to 190°C (375°F), Gas Mark 5 and bake the fish, uncovered, for 25 minutes.

Serve hot with mixed vegetables or cold with salad.

Devilled Pilchards

Preparation time: 15 minutes

Cooking time: 12 minutes

Quantity: 4 helpings

Canned pilchards are low on points and sustaining.

1 tablespoon mustard powder
1 tablespoon vinegar
1 tablespoon sugar
1 oz (25 g) margarine or dripping, melted
1 x 15 oz (425 g) can pilchards
1 small onion, finely chopped
1 bay leaf
4-6 cloves or good pinch ground cloves
¼ pint (150 ml) liquid (see method)
chopped fresh parsley, to garnish

Blend the mustard with the vinegar, sugar and half the melted margarine or dripping. Lift the pilchards from the can, split and spread with the mustard mixture then fold over again. Save the liquid from the can.

Place the fish in the grill pan, or a suitable dish, and put under a preheated grill for a few minutes while making the sauce.

Heat the remaining margarine or dripping, add the onion and cook for 2 minutes, put in the bay leaf and cloves. Tip the liquid from the can into a measure, add enough water to give ¼ pint (150 ml). Pour over the onion and simmer 5 minutes. Remove the bay leaf and cloves. Spoon the sauce over the fish and return to the grill for 5 minutes. Garnish with parsley and serve.

Fish and Tomato Bake

PREPARATION TIME: 15 MINUTES

COOKING TIME: 30 MINUTES

QUANTITY: 4 HELPINGS

The tomatoes in this dish keep the fish beautifully moist. No fat is needed in the dish at all.

1 lb (450 g) tomatoes, sliced
1 teaspoon sugar
salt and pepper
2 tablespoons chopped parsley
2 tablespoons chopped spring onions
½ teaspoon chopped thyme or ¼ teaspoon dried thyme
4 white fish cutlets
3 tablespoons crisp browned breadcrumbs

Preheat the oven to 180°C (350°F), Gas Mark 4. Place half the sliced tomatoes in a flat layer at the bottom of a shallow casserole or large pie dish.

Blend the sugar, seasoning, parsley, spring onions and thyme together. Add a sprinkling of this mixture to the tomatoes. Arrange the fish cutlets in a layer over the tomatoes, and flavour them with some more of the herb mixture. Cover with the remaining tomatoes and the last of the herb mixture. Top with the bread-crumbs and bake in the preheated oven for 30 minutes.

Serve the fish bake hot with seasonal vegetables, including a green leaf vegetable, if possible.

Variation: When fresh tomatoes are not available use bottled tomato purée.

Scalloped Herrings

This is a good way to use up leftover fish and potatoes.

Bone, skin and flake 2 small cooked herrings; mix into ½ pint (300 ml) white sauce. Grease a shallow dish and sprinkle over it 2 tablespoons breadcrumbs. Spoon the fish mixture into the dish and top with 8 oz (225 g) mashed potato. Sprinkle on another 2 tablespoons breadcrumbs and dot with ½ oz (15 g) margarine. Bake in a hot oven, 200°C (400°F) Gas Mark 6 for about 25 minutes, until browned on top.

Fish Soufflé

Preparation time: 20 minutes

Cooking time: 40 minutes

Quantity: 4 helpings

A soufflé is an ideal dish for a special celebration. You can make this, even if you have no fresh eggs, for reconstituted dried eggs are an acceptable alternative.

8 oz (225 g) white fish
1 oz (25 g) margarine
1 oz (25 g) flour
¼ pint (150 ml) milk or fish stock
few drops anchovy essence (optional)
3-4 reconstituted dried eggs or fresh eggs
salt and pepper

Preheat the oven to 190°C (375°F), Gas Mark 5. Grease a 6-7 inch (15-18 cm) soufflé dish or a small casserole with a little margarine.

Make sure the fish is free from skin and bone. While cooked fish can be used, a stronger favour is given if you use uncooked white fish. Either mince or chop it, then pound it very well. If using cooked fish flake it finely.

Heat the margarine in a saucepan, stir in the flour, then gradually add the milk or stock. Stir or whisk briskly as the sauce comes to the boil and becomes very thick. Add the anchovy essence, if using. Blend the fish with hot sauce then remove the pan from the heat.

With dried eggs: reconstitute the eggs in the usual way and whisk into the fish mixture, season to taste.

With fresh eggs: separate the yolks and whites. Whisk the yolks into the fish mixture, season to taste. Whisk the egg whites until they stand in peaks, do not over-whip them, for that makes a dry soufflé. Fold into the other ingredients.

Spoon the mixture into the soufflé dish and bake for 30 minutes, or until well-risen and golden in colour. Serve at once.

MEAT DISHES

When a family was planning a Victory Celebration Meal, everyone would probably save their meat ration coupons to buy a good-sized joint (they would manage without meat for many days to do this).

The meat ration was 1s 2d worth per person per week (6p in modern money) for a family of 4 people over a period of 2 weeks. A recipe list from a Ministry of Food leaflet suggesting how the meat ration could be best used over the two weeks, was based on the family's buying just one joint in that time; for the second week, dishes such as Fillets of lamb, based on breast of lamb, or Stuffed marrow were suggested.

At the time this leaflet was published liver, which had previously been included on the meat ration due to a shortage of other meats, was just taken off the ration, as supplies has improved.

LIVER AND BACON HOT-POT

Preparation time: 25 minutes

Cooking time: 45 minutes

Quantity: 4-6 helpings

When not on the ration liver was greatly in demand; people would queue at the butcher's shop, hoping the supply would last until it was their turn to be served. This dish would often be served with dumplings, cooked separately from the hot-pot.

1 lb (450 g) lambs' liver
salt and pepper
3 bacon rashers
1 tablespoon flour
8 oz (225 g) carrots, thinly sliced

Put the liver into a pan of cold salted water, bring just to the boil, then drain, saving about ½ pint (300 ml) of the water. When cool, slice the liver thinly.

Grill the bacon, then derind and chop it.

Season the flour and coat the liver and bacon. Pack the meat into a casserole with the carrots and the reserved ½ pint (300 ml) stock. Cover the casserole, put it in a preheated oven, 180°C (350°F) Gas Mark 4 and bake for 35-40 minutes.

If liked, make dumplings to serve with the hot-pot.

FILLETS OF LAMB

PREPARATION TIME: 30 MINUTES

COOKING TIME: 1 HOUR PLUS 15 MINUTES ON THE SECOND DAY

QUANTITY: 4 HELPINGS ON 2 DAYS

Here, two breasts of lamb are used to give two meals, each providing small portions for 4 people.

2 flaps of breast of lamb
salt
2-3 carrots, sliced
1 small turnip, sliced
1 bay leaf
2-3 peppercorns
blade of mace
few parsley stalks
little mint sauce
little made mustard

Trim away the surplus fat from the breasts, then score round the small bones with a sharp knife. Do not remove the bones. Place the meat in a pan of boiling salted water with the vegetables and the herbs, tied in muslin. If fresh herbs are not available use ½-1 teaspoon mixed dried herbs.

Cover the pan and simmer gently for 1 hour, when the meat should be tender and easy to loosen from the bones. Put the meat on a board and remove the bones.

Spread both inner sides of the meat with the mint sauce and mustard. Set one breast of meat in a straight-sided baking tin, then place the second breast over it, with the coated side inside. Press well together, keep in position with a second tin, well weighted down. Leave in a cool place overnight in this position.

Meal 1 Cut half the breasts into neat thin fingers and serve cold with salad and mixed vegetables.

Meal 2 Cut the remaining lamb into neat fingers, coat in batter or egg and breadcrumbs and fry in a little hot fat until crisp and brown.

Mock Goose

PREPARATION TIME: 25 MINUTES

COOKING TIME: 1 HOUR

QUANTITY: 6-8 HELPINGS

Among the many war-time recipes for making Mock Duck and Mock Goose, this one, which could used either mutton or lamb, was ideal for special occasions.

1 leg of mutton or lamb, boned
For the stuffing:
2-3 medium onions or 4 large leeks, finely chopped
2 small cooking apples, peeled, cored and chopped
3 oz (75 g) breadcrumbs
2-3 teaspoons chopped sage or 1-1½ teaspoons dried sage
1 oz (25 g) margarine, melted
salt and pepper

Spread the boned meat out flat. Blend all the stuffing ingredients together. Put over the meat, then roll up and form into the shape of the body of a goose. Tie securely. Weigh the joint to calculate the cooking time and roast it as usual.

VEGETABLE AND KIDNEY PIE

PREPARATION TIME: 30 MINUTES

COOKING TIME: 55 MINUTES

QUANTITY: 4 HELPINGS

2-3 lb (1-1.5 kg) mixed vegetables
salt and pepper
1-2 tomatoes, if available
4 oz (100 g) ox kidney or 2 sheep's kidneys
For the gravy:
1½ oz (40 g) flour, preferably wheatmeal
1 pint (600 ml) vegetable stock
1 teaspoon yeast extract or vegetable extract
Wheatmeal pastry (page 23)

Peel and dice root vegetables, pod peas and cut beans into small pieces. Put the root vegetables and any other vegetables that are not young and tender, into boiling lightly salted water and cook for 10 minutes only; strain and save the vegetable water for the gravy. Slice the tomatoes, if using, and mix with the other vegetables.

Skin the ox or sheep's kidney(s), remove the core. Cut into very thin slices. Put into a little well-seasoned water and simmer for 15 minutes, then strain.

Pack the kidney and vegetables in layers in a 2-3 pint (1.2-1.8 litre) pie dish. Blend the flour with the vegetable water and extract then cook steadily until a thickened gravy. Pour gravy to cover the vegetables into the pie dish, saving the rest to serve with the meal. Allow to cool before covering the filling with pastry.

Make the pastry and use to cover the pie.

Preheat the oven to 190°C (375°F), Gas Mark 5 and bake the pie for 45 minutes. Lower the heat slightly after 30 minutes if the pastry is becoming a little too brown. Serve hot with the rest of the gravy.

Variation: If using lamb's kidneys there is no need to pre-cook them; simply skin, core and dice finely.

VEGETABLE MINCE

Preparation time: 30 minutes

Cooking time: 40 minutes

Quantity: 4 helpings

This Ministry of Food recipe illustrates how a small amount of meat and a generous amount of vegetables could provide a satisfying meal.

1 lb (450 g) small potatoes
1-1½ lb (450-675 g) carrots
salt and pepper
1 lb (450 g) green peas
1 oz (25 g) dripping or fat
1 large tomato, sliced
1 large onion, or equivalent spring onions
4-6 oz (100-175 g) minced beef
½ oz (15 g) flour
little vegetable stock

Put the potatoes and carrots into boiling salted water and cook steadily for 20 minutes then add the peas and continue cooking for a further 15 minutes.

Meanwhile heat the dripping in a pan, add the tomato and onion(s) and cook gently for 10 minutes, add the minced beef, blend with the vegetables and stir with a fork to keep the meat crumbly. Stir over a low heat for a further 10 minutes then add the flour and enough vegetable stock to make a sauce-like consistency. Season the mixture, bring to the boil and cook gently for 5-10 minutes. Dish up the vegetables in a deep hot dish and top with the mince.

Wheatmeal Pastry

Wheatmeal flour makes very good pastry but, because it is a little heavier than white flour, you should add a small amount of baking powder.

Blend 8 oz (225 g) plain wheatmeal flour with ½ teaspoon salt and 1 teaspoon baking powder.

Rub in 2 oz (50 g) margarine or cooking fat or dripping then add enough water to make a rolling consistency, although one that is slightly softer than when making pastry with white flour.

Roll out and use as in the individual recipe.

MINCE-STUFFED MARROW

Preparation time: 25 minutes

Cooking time: 1 hour

Quantity: 4 helpings

3 oz (75 g) bread, preferably wheatmeal
¼ pint (150 ml) water
4 spring onions, if possible, chopped
2 teaspoons chopped fresh herbs or ½ teaspoon mixed dried herbs
4-6 oz (100-175 g) raw minced beef
salt and pepper
1 medium marrow
1 oz (25 g) dripping or fat

Put the bread into a basin, add the water. Leave to soak for 5 minutes then beat until smooth, add the chopped spring onions (if available), the fresh or dried herbs, minced beef and seasoning.

Wipe the marrow. Cut into half, lengthways, scoop out the seeds and fill with the stuffing. Put the two halves together, tie firmly with tape or string.

Preheat the oven to 180°C (350°F), Gas Mark 4 and melt the dripping or fat in a roasting tin. Add the marrow and turn around in the hot fat. Bake for 1 hour, basting from time to time with the fat in the tin.

Serve with mixed vegetables.

Variation: Add extra ingredients to this basic recipe: 2 skinned and chopped tomatoes, 4 oz (100 g) sliced mushrooms, 4-8 extra spring onions (or use 1-2 onions, chopped and cooked for 5 minutes in hot fat).

BLANQUETTE OF CHICKEN

PREPARATION TIME: 30 MINUTES

COOKING TIME: 2½ HOURS

QUANTITY: 4-6 HELPINGS

Most war-time chickens were elderly, with plenty of fat, which would be rendered down to use in cooking.

1 boiling fowl
3 onions or leeks, left whole
4 medium carrots, left whole
1 turnip, diced
salt and pepper
small bunch of mixed herbs or ½ teaspoon dried mixed herbs
For the sauce:
1 oz (25 g) margarine (see method)
1 oz (25 g) flour
¼ pint (150 ml) milk
½ pint (300 ml) chicken stock
1 or 2 reconstituted dried or fresh eggs
chopped parsley

Put the chicken into a large saucepan with the vegetables. Add sufficient water to cover and a little seasoning. Add the herbs, securely tied in muslin. Bring the liquid to boiling point, cover the pan and simmer for 2½ hours, or until the chicken is tender.

Towards the end of the cooking time make the sauce. If you are very short of margarine, omit it and rely on the fat in the chicken stock to give the right flavour to the sauce. Measure out the stock from the pan in which the chicken is cooking, then strain it..

If using margarine: heat in a pan, stir in the flour then add the milk and most of the stock and bring to the boil and cook until thickened. If not using margarine: blend the flour with the milk and most of the stock, bring to the boil and cook until thickened. Remove the pan from the heat so the sauce is no longer boiling.

Beat the dried or fresh egg(s) with the remaining cold stock, whisk into the sauce and simmer gently for 2 or 3 minutes.

Serve the chicken and vegetables with the sauce.

Variation: use the cooked chicken and sauce to make a chicken mould. Dice the chicken meat and pack into a mould. Dissolve 2 teaspoons gelatine in the hot sauce, pour over the chicken and leave to set.

BLACK PUDDING HOT-POT

PREPARATION TIME: 20 MINUTES

COOKING TIME: 1 HOUR

QUANTITY: 4 HELPINGS.

8 oz (225 g) black pudding
8 oz (225 g) potatoes, thinly sliced
8 oz (225 g) carrots, thinly sliced
1 large onion, if available, finely chopped
1 teaspoon chopped sage or ½ teaspoon dried sage
1 oz (25 g) flour
1 teaspoon gravy powder
¾ pint (450 ml) water
salt and pepper

Skin the black pudding and cut into ¼ inch (5 mm) slices. Arrange a layer of sliced potatoes in a greased casserole, then a layer of black pudding and carrots. Blend the onion and sage, sprinkle half into the casserole. Add another layer of carrots then the black pudding and chopped onion and sage. End with a layer of sliced potatoes. Blend the flour, gravy powder and water together in a pan and stir over heat until thickened, add a little seasoning. Pour over the ingredients in the casserole and cover with a lid. Preheat the oven to 180°C (350°F), Gas Mark 4 and bake the casserole for 1 hour.

This nutritious casserole is good served with sliced cooked beetroot.

Sheep's Head Roll

PREPARATION TIME: 45 MINUTES COOKING TIME: 2½-3 HOURS QUANTITY: 6-8 HELPINGS

If you have never cooked sheep's head before you will be delighted at the amount of meat you can obtain from it and the tasty flavour of the roll. The vegetables make the meat go further, as well as adding flavour.

1 sheep's head
salt and pepper
1 tablespoon vinegar
2 dried cloves or pinch ground cloves
1 blade of mace
pinch ground cinnamon
1 garlic clove, chopped
1 tablespoon chopped mixed herbs or ½ teaspoon mixed dried herbs
1 lb (450 g) turnips, diced
1 lb (450 g) carrots, diced
4 oz (100 g) brown breadcrumbs
4 oz (100 g) flour

Soak the sheep's head in salted water for a short time, remove and put into a saucepan with cold water to cover. Bring the water to the boil, then discard it. This is known as 'blanching' and it gives a better colour and flavour to the meat.

Tie the head in a cloth, this makes sure the delicate brains, which are so nourishing, are kept with the head in cooking. Return the head to the saucepan with fresh water to cover, and the vinegar, spices, herbs and vegetables. Season lightly. Cover the pan and simmer steadily for 1½-2 hours, or until the head is sufficiently tender to remove the meat.

Strain the stock and put the head and vegetables on one side. Remove the meat from the head and thinly slice the tongue. Keep this separate. Mince or finely chop the rest of the meat, blend with the softened vegetables, the breadcrumbs and the flour. Season to taste.

Press the meat mixture into a long strip with floured hands, arrange the sliced tongue down the centre and then form into a roll. Either wrap this in margarine paper and a cloth or put into a large greased jam jar. Steam for 1 hour.

Allow to become cold, then unwrap or turn out of the jar, slice and serve with salad.

Variations: Coat the cooked roll with browned breadcrumbs before serving.

Add a little tomato ketchup or Worcestershire sauce to the meat mixture to give additional flavour.

Although the roll is generally served as a cold dish it is equally good hot with a gravy, made from some of the stock used in cooking the beef.

VEGETABLE DISHES

Vegetables became very important during the years of shortages and most people found adventurous ways of cooking them. For celebration meals, trouble would be taken to make them as interesting as possible.

CHEESE, TOMATO AND POTATO LOAF

PREPARATION TIME: 30 MINUTES

COOKING TIME: 35 MINUTES

QUANTITY: 4 HELPINGS

1 lb (450 g) cooked new potatoes
12 oz (350 g) tomatoes
1 oz (25 g) margarine
1 oz (25 g) flour
7½ fl oz (225 ml) milk or milk and vegetable stock
3 oz (75 g) cheese, grated
salt and pepper
To coat the tin:
½ oz (15 g) margarine
1 oz (25 g) crisp fine breadcrumbs

Cut the potatoes into slices about ⅓ inch (7.5mm) thick. Cut the tomatoes into slightly thicker slices. Heat the margarine in a saucepan, add the flour, then the milk, or milk and vegetable water, stir or whisk briskly as the sauce comes to the boil and thickens. Remove from the heat, add the cheese and seasoning.

Grease a 2 lb (900 g) loaf tin or use an oval casserole and coat with the breadcrumbs. Preheat the oven to 180°C (350°F), Gas Mark 4.

Arrange about a third of the potatoes in a neat layer in the container, cover with a little sauce and half the tomatoes. Put in half the remaining potatoes, with the rest of the sauce and tomatoes. Add a final layer of potatoes. Cover the dish with margarine paper and bake in the preheated oven for 30-35 minutes. Turn out and serve hot with a salad.

CABBAGE CASSEROLE

PREPARATION TIME: 20 MINUTES

COOKING TIME: 35 MINUTES

QUANTITY: 4 HELPINGS

It often surprises people to know it was possible to hard-boil dried eggs. Obviously they did not look like a proper egg, for white and yolk were mixed together, but they tasted perfectly pleasant.

2 tablespoons dried egg powder and 4 tablespoons water, or 2 fresh eggs
½ pint (300 ml) water
salt and pepper
1 small cabbage, shredded
salt and pepper
½ oz (15 g) margarine
1 tablespoon flour
¼ pint (150 ml) milk
4 oz (100 g) cheese, thinly sliced
2 tablespoons fine, crisped breadcrumbs

Reconstitute the eggs by blending the powder with the 4 tablespoons of cold water. Pour into a greased cup or small basin, cover with margarine paper and steam over boiling water for 10 minutes. If using fresh eggs, boil them for 10 minutes, then crack and remove the shells. Slice the dried or fresh eggs neatly.

While the eggs are cooking bring the ½ pint (300 ml)

water to the boil, add a little salt and shake of pepper, then put in the cabbage and cook for 5 minutes, then strain. The cabbage liquid can be saved as vegetable stock, for soup or vegetable dishes. Heat the margarine, stir in the flour and then the milk; bring to the boil and cook until thickened; season to taste.

Put a layer of the cabbage into a greased casserole, top with a layer of sliced cheese and half the sliced eggs. Add a second layer of cabbage, cheese and eggs and then a final layer of cabbage. Top with the white sauce, then the breadcrumbs. Do not cover the casserole.

Preheat the oven to 180°C (350°F), Gas Mark 4 and bake the casserole for 25 minutes.

BEETROOT FRICASSEE

Preparation time: 20 minutes

Cooking time: 5-10 minutes

Quantity: 4-6 helpings

1 oz (25 g) margarine
1 lb (450 g) cooked beetroot, peeled and cut into 1 inch (2.5 cm) dice
1 medium onion, finely chopped
1 teaspoon flour
3 tablespoons vinegar
2 tablespoons water
salt and pepper
3 tablespoons chopped parsley

Heat the margarine in a saucepan, add the rest of the ingredients, except the parsley. Mix thoroughly and heat for 5-10 minutes only, add half the parsley, stir to blend. Top with the rest of the parsley and serve.

This fricassée is particularly good served with fish dishes, especially white fish.

Variation: Cucumber Fricassée: If you can spare cucumbers use them, peeled and diced, instead of the diced beetroot. You will need the same amount of cucumber as beetroot.

POTATO RING

Preparation time: 20 minutes

Cooking time: 45 minutes

Quantity: 4 helpings

3 large potatoes
1 tablespoon flour
1 tablespoon chopped parsley or 1 teaspoon chopped mixed herbs
salt and pepper
1 oz (25 g) cooking fat or dripping, melted

Preheat the oven to 180°C (350°F), Gas Mark 4. Scrub, but do not peel, the potatoes. Grate on a coarse grater then mix with the flour, parsley or mixed herbs and salt and pepper to taste.

Form into a ring shape on a flat baking tray or ovenproof serving dish. Brush with the melted fat or dripping and bake for 45 minutes.

When cooked, fill the centre with a mixture of cooked seasonal vegetables.

CURRIED CARROTS

Preparation time: 20 minutes

Cooking time: 20 minutes

Quantity: 4-6 helpings

2 lb (900 g) carrots, sliced
salt and pepper
1 oz (25 g) cooking fat or dripping
2 medium onions, finely chopped
1 oz (25 g) flour
1 tablespoon curry powder, or to taste
2 oz (50 g) sultanas
1 tablespoon chutney

Put the carrots into 1 pint (600 ml) boiling salted water and cook steadily for 10 minutes or until just tender.

Meanwhile, start to make the sauce. Heat the fat or

dripping in a pan, add the onions and fry steadily for a few minutes, until tender. Add the flour and curry powder, blend with the onions and cook for 1 minute.

Strain the carrots, keep hot in a warmed serving dish. Measure out ¾ pint (450 ml) of the carrot liquid, blend with the flour and onion mixture. Bring to the boil and stir over the heat until thickened, then add seasoning, sultanas and chutney. Blend well and simmer for 5 minutes. Pour over the carrots and serve.

SUMMER VEGETABLE PIE

Preparation time: 35 minutes
Cooking time: 45-50 minutes
Quantity: 4-6 helpings

This pie is excellent made with early, quite small root vegetables and tomatoes.

1 lb (450 g) carrots, sliced
8 oz (225 g) turnips, cut into ½ inch (1.5 cm) dice
8 oz (225 g) parsnips, cut into ½ inch (1.5 cm) dice
8 oz (225 g) onions, finely chopped
¾ pint (450 ml) water
salt and pepper
1 lb (450 g) tomatoes, sliced
2 oz (50 g) margarine
1½ oz (40 g) flour
¼ pint (150 ml) milk
2 oz (50 g) cheese, grated
2 large slices of bread, 1 inch (2.5 cm) thick

Put the carrots, turnips, parsnips and onions into the water, add salt and cook until just tender, do not overcook. Strain and keep ½ pint (300 ml) of the stock.

Arrange the mixed vegetables with the sliced tomatoes in a 2½ pint (1.5 litre) greased pie dish. Preheat the oven to 190°C (375°F), Gas Mark 5.

Heat 1 oz (25 g) margarine in a saucepan, stir in the flour, then add the milk and vegetable stock. Bring to the boil and stir or whisk until thickened and smooth. Add seasoning to taste. Remove from the heat and stir in the cheese. Spoon over the vegetables.

Cut the bread into 1 inch (2.5 cm) dice. Put on top of the vegetable mixture. Melt the remaining margarine and spoon over the bread. Bake in the preheated oven for 20-25 minutes or until the topping is crisp and brown. Serve hot.

TOMATO CHARLOTTE

Preparation time: 15 minutes
Cooking time: 30 minutes
Quantity: 4 helpings

This recipe can be served as a light main dish topped with grated cheese, or as a vegetable with meat or fish, in which case omit the cheese.

salt and pepper
2 teaspoons sugar
1¼ lb (55 g) tomatoes, thinly sliced
4 oz (100 g) breadcrumbs
2 tablespoons chopped parsley
2 tablespoons chopped chives or spring onions
1 oz (25 g) margarine or dripping melted

Preheat the oven to 180°C (350°F), Gas Mark 4. Grease a 1½ pint (900 ml) pie dish. Blend a little seasoning with the sugar and sprinkle over the tomatoes. Arrange layers of breadcrumbs and tomatoes in the dish, ending with breadcrumbs. Add most of the parsley and chives or spring onions to the tomato layers but save a little for garnish. Top with the margarine or dripping and bake for 30 minutes. Sprinkle with the parsley and chives or spring onions; serve hot.

Variation: Add 1½-3 oz (40-75 g) grated cheese to the breadcrumb topping or chopped spring onions or chopped fresh parsley.

Puddings were a very essential part of most meals for they helped to satisfy hungry people. In summer most people based their puddings on seasonal fruits. In cold weather steamed puddings were popular.

Marmalade Pudding

PREPARATION TIME: 25 MINUTES

COOKING TIME: 1½ HOURS

QUANTITY: 4-6 HELPINGS

This recipe for a very satisfying pudding is an ideal way to use up stale bread.

1 oz (25 g) margarine
¼ pint (150 ml) milk or milk and water
4 oz (100 g) bread
1 oz (25 g) self-raising or plain flour
1 teaspoon baking powder
1 oz (25 g) sugar
3 tablespoons marmalade
1 reconstituted or fresh egg

Heat the margarine with the milk, or milk and water. Crumble the bread into a basin, add the hot milk and melted margarine, blend well, then allow to stand for 10 minutes. Sift the flour and baking powder into the bread mixture, then add the sugar, half the marmalade and the egg. Beat well until you have a smooth mixture.

Grease a 1½ pint (900 ml) pudding basin, put the rest of the marmalade at the bottom of the basin, then add the pudding mixture. Cover with margarine paper and steam for 1½ hours. Turn the pudding out and serve it with custard (page 38).

Bird's Nest Pudding

PREPARATION TIME: 25 MINUTES

COOKING TIME: 1¼ HOURS

QUANTITY: 4 HELPINGS

Tapioca was the preferred cereal for this pudding.

2 oz (50 g) tapioca
1 pint (600 ml) milk, or milk and water
1-2 oz (25-50 g) sugar
4 medium cooking apples, peeled and cored
8 teaspoons jam or bramble jelly

Put the tapioca, milk and sugar into a saucepan, stir over a low heat until the mixture thickens, then cook for 10 minutes.

Place the apples in a large pie dish. Preheat the oven to 160°C (325°F), Gas Mark 3. Fill the centre of the apples with the jam or jelly. Pour the thickened milk pudding around the apples and bake in the preheated oven for 50-60 minutes, or until the apples are tender.

Mocha Foam

This is like a mousse. It may be served by itself or as a topping on a plain cake or dessert.

¼ pint (150 ml) moderately strong coffee
1 teaspooon gelatine
1 tablespoon cocoa powder
1 oz (25 g) sugar
3 tablespoons dried milk powder

Put 3 tablespoons of the cold coffee into a basin and add the gelatine. Allow to stand for 2 minutes then melt over a pan of hot, but not boiling, water. Heat the rest of the coffee, add the cocoa powder, sugar and dissolved gelatine. Gradually whisk in the dried milk powder (make sure there are no lumps) and continue whisking until light and fluffy.

Fruit Amber

Preparation time: 25 minutes

Cooking time: 40 minutes, but see method

Quantity: 4 helpings

This is a very good way to make a special pudding with a relatively small amount of fruit. If you can spare fresh eggs then the pudding can have a meringue on top.

12 oz (350 g) fruit
little water (see method)
1-2 oz (25-50 g) sugar, or to taste
2 oz (50 g) soft breadcrumbs
2 reconstituted dried eggs
¼ pint (150 ml) milk

Heat the oven to 160°C (325°F), Gas Mark 3. Prepare the fruit. Apples should be peeled, cored and sliced; plums can be halved and stoned.

If using very firm fruit, such as apples or plums, pre-cook them for a short time in a saucepan with 2-3 tablespoons water and sugar to taste. The fruit should be almost, but not quite, cooked, then it should be mashed to make a purée.

With soft fruit all you need to do is mash this, without pre-cooking, to make a purée.

Blend the sugar with the fruit, if this has not been used in cooking, add the breadcrumbs and mix well. Whisk the eggs and milk together and add to the other ingredients.

Grease a 1½ pint (900 ml) pie dish, add the fruit mixture and bake in the preheated oven for 35 minutes, or until firm. Serve as soon as possible after baking.

Variation: If using 2 fresh eggs, add the yolks only to the fruit mixture. Bake the pudding as above. When it is firm, lower the heat to 150°C (300°F), Gas Mark 2. Whisk the 2 egg whites until stiff, fold in 2 oz (50 g) sugar. Spoon over the pudding and bake for 25 minutes or until golden in colour. Serve hot.

Toffee Apple Pudding

Preparation time: 25 minutes

Cooking time: 2 hours

Quantity: 4-6 helpings

This was a steamed pudding to serve for a special treat or on a special occasion.

For coating the basin:
1 oz (25 g) margarine
2 tablespoons brown sugar
For the pudding:
8 oz (225 g) self-raising flour or plain flour sifted with 2 teaspoons baking powder
pinch salt
2 teaspoons sugar
2 oz (50 g) margarine
water to bind
1 lb (450 g) cooking apples, peeled, cored and thinly sliced
sugar to sweeten
2 tablespoons water

Spread the margarine for coating inside a 2 pint (1.2 litre) basin, then add the sugar, making sure this adheres to the margarine.

Sift the flour, or flour and baking powder, with the salt and sugar into a bowl. Rub in the margarine, then add sufficient water to make a soft dough. Roll out three-quarters of the dough and use to line the basin. Add the apples, a little sugar and the water. Damp the edges of the pastry with water. Roll out the remaining pastry to form the lid, place over the filling and seal the edges firmly.

Cover with margarine paper and a cloth and steam over rapidly boiling water for 1 hour, then lower the heat and cook steadily for a further hour. Turn out and serve hot with custard (page 38).

☆ ☆ ☆ ☆ ☆ ☆

THRIFTY CHRISTMAS PUDDING

Preparation time: 35 minutes

Cooking time: 2½ hours plus another 1 hour

Quantity: 6 helpings

I demonstrated this recipe just before Christmas 1944. The rolled oats give a nutty texture and the carrots help to save sugar as well as improve the colour of the mixture.

3 oz (75 g) bread, weight without crusts
¼ pint (150 ml) water
3 oz (75 g) plain flour
1½ teaspoons baking powder
½ teaspoon mixed spice
½ teaspoon ground cinnamon
3 oz (75 g) rolled oats
3 oz (75 g) carrots, finely grated
3 oz (75 g) margarine, melted
3 oz (75 g) sugar, preferably brown
8 oz (225 g) mixed dried fruit
2 fresh or reconstituted dried eggs

Break the bread into small pieces, put into the cold water and leave for at least 20 minutes then beat with a fork until smooth. Sift the flour with the baking powder and spices, add to the bread with the rest of the ingredients and mix thoroughly.

Grease a 2½ pint (1.5 litre) basin, spoon in the mixture. Cover carefully with margarine paper then a cloth or greaseproof paper and steam over boiling water for 2½ hours. Remove the damp covers, leave to dry then replace on the pudding. Store in a cool place for 2-3 days only. On Christmas morning, steam for 1 hour. Traditionally, the pudding would be served with Sherry Custard or Hard Sauce.

☆ ☆ ☆ ☆ ☆ ☆

CHRISTMAS CHOCOLATE LOG

Preparation time: 20 minutes

Cooking time: 12-15 minutes

Quantity: Makes 1 cake

While the National flour made it impossible to produce a really lighter sponge, this was quite acceptable.

3 reconstituted dried eggs or 3 shell eggs
3-4 oz (75-100 g) sugar, preferably caster
3 oz (75 g) self-raising flour or plain flour sifted with ¾ teaspoon baking powder
1 oz (25 g) margarine, melted
For the filling:
little jam
For the coating:
2 oz (50 g) margarine
4 oz (100 g) icing sugar, sifted
1 tablespoon cocoa powder, sifted

Preheat the oven to 190°C (375°F), Gas Mark 5. Line a Swiss Roll tin approximately 9 x 11 inches (23 x 28 cm) with greased greaseproof paper.

Put the eggs and most of the sugar into a bowl and whisk until thick and creamy. Sift the flour, or flour and baking powder, twice to lighten it. Fold gently into the egg and sugar mixture, then fold in the margarine. Spoon into the prepared tin. Bake in the preheated oven for 12-15 minutes, or until firm to a gentle touch.

Sprinkle a sheet of greaseproof paper with the rest of the sugar. Turn the sponge out on to this, remove the cooking paper. Spread with the jam and roll firmly. Leave until cold.

Cream the margarine for the filling until soft, add most of the icing sugar and all the cocoa. Mix thoroughly then spread over the roll, mark ridges with a fork to look like a tree trunk. Sprinkle the last of the icing sugar over the log. Decorate the serving plate with fresh holly.

STREET PARTIES

Street parties were the most popular way of celebrating the Victory Days in 1945. Some parties were exclusively for children, with adults waiting on table. Other parties would be for everyone living in the street, often with the visiting milkman, postman, air-raid wardens or anyone known to the inhabitants asked to join in. There were also special street parties for the elderly.

The typical street party recipes here are in relatively small quantities, for volunteers would undertake either to make some of the dishes needed or to donate a precious pat of fat, a little of their tea ration or a pot of jam.

People who were children in 1945 have told me that they had ice cream at their street party - the first time they had ever tasted it. Sometimes it could have been home-made, but relatively few people had refrigerators in the 1940s, so it seems it must have come from caterers or shops who either had refrigerators or made the ice cream with available ingredients in old-fashioned ice cream makers. There is a wartime ice cream recipe on page 39, suitable for making in a refrigerator or an ice cream maker.

MENU FOR CHILDREN'S STREET PARTIES

Sandwiches (this page)
Sausage Rolls (page 42)
Selection of cakes, tarts and biscuits
Jellies (page 38)
Ice cream, if available (page 39)
Lemon and orange squash
Milk and/or tea

MENU FOR CHILDREN'S AND ADULTS' STREET PARTIES

Sandwiches (this page)
Victory Scotch Eggs (page 35)
Beef Shortcakes (page 35)
Selection of cakes, tarts and biscuits
Jellies for the children (page 38)
Ice cream, if available (page 39)
Celebration Trifle (page 38)
Lemon and orange squash
Beer and cider
Milk and tea

MENU FOR THE ELDERLY

Home-made soup (pages 14-15)
Ham and Beef Roll (page 36)
or selection of cold meats
Various salads (pages 16-17)
Celebration Trifle (page 38)
Fruit salads
Orange and Date Cake (pages 36-7)
Beer and other drinks
Tea

SANDWICHES

These are some of the sandwich fillings that could be made to celebrate VE and VJ days in 1945. Foods such as salmon would be canned and were purchased on the points system. Two tips for sandwich making:

To make margarine go further, cream it with a little warm (not too hot) milk; this also enables it to be spread more easily and sparingly.

Cut the loaf lengthways, to save time, then cut the long slices into smaller pieces when the sandwiches have been made.

FOR YOUNGER CHILDREN

Jam and Mock Lemon Curd (page 39) were favourite sweet fillings. Potted meat or fish were usual savoury ones. In addition there could be:

Mock banana sandwiches: cook parsnips until very soft; drain well then mash until very smooth with a few drops of banana essence and a little sugar.

Cheese and date spread: blend finely grated cheese and mix with chopped dates.

Cheese and carrot: blend equal quantities of grated raw carrot and grated cheese; moisten with a little milk or one of the mayonnaise recipes on page 17.

Egg sandwiches: scramble reconstituted or fresh eggs in a little margarine, cool, blend with mayonnaise (see page 17) and put on shredded lettuce or watercress.

FOR ADULTS AND OLDER CHILDREN

Pilchard and cucumber: mix mashed pilchards and finely diced or grated cucumber, serve on lettuce or shredded cabbage heart. For salmon and cucumber, use salmon in place of pilchards.

Salad sandwiches: mix sliced tomatoes, cucumber, lettuce and top with mayonnaise (page 17).

Spiced beef: flake corned beef finely, mix with a little finely chopped mustard pickle and serve on shredded red or green cabbage.

Victory Scotch Eggs

PREPARATION TIME: 20 MINUTES

COOKING TIME: 40 MINUTES

QUANTITY: MAKES 8 HALVES

This is a special version of the well-known savoury. When making these to serve as one of the savoury dishes for a Victory Party you can cut the halved eggs into smaller pieces so they go further.

4 shell eggs
2 oz (50 g) cheese, grated
1 tablespoon Mayonnaise (page 17)
1 lb (450 g) sausagemeat
To coat:
little reconstituted dried egg or shell egg or milk
2 oz (50 g) crisp breadcrumbs

Boil the shell eggs for 10 minutes, then shell and cut in halves across the eggs. Cool sufficiently to handle then carefully remove the egg yolks. Mash these in a basin, then add the cheese and mayonnaise. Spoon into the white cases and press the egg halves together firmly.

Divide the sausagemeat into 4 portions, wrap around the eggs, seal the joins very firmly. Brush with a little egg or milk then coat with the crisp breadcrumbs.

Preheat the oven to 190°C (375°F), Gas Mark 5. As the oven is heating put in a greased baking tray to become very hot. Put the Scotch Eggs on the hot tray and bake in the preheated oven for 30 minutes. To serve, cut into halves or quarters. Garnish with lettuce.

Variations: Omit the cheese and mayonnaise to make the usual Scotch Eggs.

Use reconstituted dried eggs, steaming them in 4 very small cups. Mash the cooked eggs, add the cheese and mayonnaise. Shape into rounds then coat with the sausagemeat and continue as the recipe.

Beef Shortcakes

PREPARATION TIME: 25 MINUTES

COOKING TIME: 25 MINUTES

QUANTITY: 12 TO 16 SHORTCAKES

These shortcakes are equally good hot or cold. If serving hot prepare the filling while the shortcakes are baking. Split the shortcakes, add the filling and serve as soon as possible. If serving cold, then cool both the shortcakes and the filling before putting them together.

For the shortcakes:
12 oz (350 g) self-raising flour or plain flour sifted with 3 teaspoons baking powder
½ teaspoon salt
1 teaspoon mustard powder, if available
2 oz (50 g) margarine or fat
milk, or milk and water, to bind
For the filling:
1 oz (25 g) margarine
1 oz (25 g) plain flour
¼ pint (150 ml) milk
4 tablespoons left-over gravy, if available
8-10 oz (225-300 g) corned beef
1 teaspoon Worcestershire sauce
salt and pepper

Preheat the oven to 220°C (425°F), Gas Mark 7. Lightly grease a baking tray.

Sift the flour, or flour and baking powder, with the salt and mustard powder. Rub in the margarine or fat then bind to a soft consistency with the milk, or milk and water. Roll out the dough to ¾ inch (1.5 cm) thick and cut into 12-16 rounds. Put on to the baking tray and cook for 12-15 minutes, or until quite firm.

Heat the margarine for the filling, stir in the flour, then add the milk and stir briskly as the sauce comes to the boil and thickens. Add the gravy; if none is available see the suggestions below.

Flake the corned beef, add to the sauce with the

Worcestershire sauce and a little seasoning.

Split the shortcakes, spread the bottom halves with the filling, then cover with the top halves.

Variations: When no gravy is available add 2 fresh skinned and chopped tomatoes or 2 well-drained chopped bottled tomatoes or use a little extra milk or vegetable stock in the sauce.

Instead of corned beef finely chop or mince any cooked meat you have.

If serving the shortcakes cold, put a layer of crisp lettuce or shredded cabbage heart on the shortcake before adding the filling.

Ham and Beef Roll

PREPARATION TIME: 20 MINUTES

COOKING TIME: 2 HOURS

QUANTITY: 4-6 HELPINGS

4 oz (100 g) fat ham, minced
1 lb (450 g) lean beef, minced
2 oz (50 g) soft breadcrumbs
1 teaspoon finely chopped sage or ½ teaspoon dried sage
1 reconstituted dried or fresh egg
salt and pepper
little flour, for shaping and coating

Blend all the ingredients but the flour together, form into a roll with floured hands. Put into a floured cloth or cover with margarine paper.

Steam for 2 hours then serve hot with gravy and seasonal vegetables or cold with salad.

Ginger Honey Buns

PREPARATION TIME: 15 MINUTES

COOKING TIME: 12-15 MINUTES

QUANTITY: 12-14 CAKES

8 oz (225 g) self-raising flour or plain flour sifted with 2 teaspoons baking powder
½-1 teaspoon ground ginger
2 oz (50 g) margarine
2 oz (50 g) sugar
2 tablespoons clear honey
2 oz (50 g) sultanas or other dried fruit
1 fresh or reconstituted dried egg
little milk or milk and water

Preheat the oven to 200°C (400°F), Gas Mark 6. Grease 2 baking trays. Sift the flour, or flour and baking powder, with the ginger. Rub in the margarine, add the sugar, honey, dried fruit, and egg. Mix well. Gradually add enough milk, or milk and water, to make a sticky dough that stands up in peaks. Put spoonfuls on the baking trays and bake in the preheated oven for 12-15 minutes, until golden and firm. Cool on a wire rack.

Orange and Date Cake

PREPARATION TIME: 15 MINUTES

COOKING TIME: 50 MINUTES

2 oz (50 g) margarine or cooking fat
2 oz (50 g) sugar
3 tablespoons orange marmalade
few drops orange essence
4 oz (100 g) dates, finely chopped
7 oz (200 g) self-raising flour, or plain flour sifted with 1¾ teaspoons baking powder
1 teaspoon ground ginger
4 tablespoons milk or water
½ teaspoon bicarbonate of soda
1 reconstituted dried or fresh egg

Preheat the oven to 160°C (325°F), Gas Mark 3. Grease and flour an oblong tin measuring about 7 x 4 inches (18 x 10 cm).

Put the margarine or cooking fat, sugar, marmalade and essence into a saucepan and stir over a low heat until melted. Remove the saucepan from the heat, add the dates to the hot mixture and allow it to stand for 15 minutes.

Sift the flour, or flour and baking powder, with the ginger, add the melted ingredients and dates then mix well. Pour the milk, or water, into the saucepan, stir to absorb any of the melted ingredients, add the bicarbonate of soda then pour on to the rest of the ingredients. Lastly add the egg. Beat well and spoon into the prepared tin. Bake the cake in the preheated oven for 50 minutes or until firm. Cool in the tin for 20 minutes then turn out on to a wire rack to cool completely.

Eggless Ginger Cake

PREPARATION TIME: 20 MINUTES

COOKING TIME: 20 MINUTES

QUANTITY: 1 CAKE

6 oz (175 g) self-raising flour or plain flour sifted with 1½ teaspoons baking powder
½-1 teaspoon ground ginger
2 oz (50 g) margarine or cooking fat
2 oz (50 g) sugar
6 tablespoons milk
¾ teaspoon bicarbonate of soda
2 teaspoons vinegar

Grease and flour a 7-8 inch (18-20 cm) cake tin. Preheat the oven to 190°C (375°F), Gas Mark 5.

Sift the flour, or flour and baking powder, with the

ginger into the mixing bowl. Rub in the margarine or fat, add the sugar and milk.

Blend the bicarbonate of soda with the vinegar: the mixture will bubble. Beat into the cake mixture. Spoon into the tin and bake for 20 minutes.

Serve the cake when fresh.

Celebration Trifle

PREPARATION TIME: 30 MINUTES

COOKING TIME: 15 MINUTES

QUANTITY: 8 HELPINGS

8 sponge squares (pages 44-5)
3-4 tablespoons jam
¼ pint (150 ml) sweet sherry
1 can or bottle of fruit in syrup
1 packet fruit jelly or 1 x recipe jelly (right)
2 pints (1.2 litres) thick custard (right)
sugar to taste
To decorate:
whipped evaporated milk (page 39) or Mock Cream (page 39)
glacé cherries
angelica

Split the sponge cakes, then sandwich them together with jam. Put into a large serving bowl.

Pour the sherry into a jug, open the can of fruit, strain enough of the syrup into the sherry to give about 7½ fl oz (225 ml). Spoon this over the sponge cakes. Chop the well-drained fruit finely and add to the sponge cakes. Measure any syrup left from the can of fruit and mix this with the liquid in which to dissolve the jelly or make a jelly from fruit squash (see right). Pour the warm jelly over the cakes and leave until set.

Make the custard. Sweeten to taste and allow to cool, whisking once or twice as it cools, so a skin does not form. Pour over the jelly and cover. When quite cold decorate with the suggested decorations.

Jelly

PREPARATION TIME: 10 MINUTES

NO COOKING

QUANTITY: 4 HELPINGS

⅔ pint (400 ml) water
1 oz (25 g) sugar
½ oz (15 g) gelatine*
⅓ pint (200 ml) fruit squash
*** this would be one sachet of today's gelatine**

Heat a little of the water with the sugar until this has dissolved. Pour 2 or 3 tablespoons of cold water into a basin, sprinkle the gelatine on top. Allow to stand for 2-3 minutes then dissolve over hot, but not boiling, water. Blend with the hot sugar and water. Add the rest of the cold water and the fruit squash. Rinse out a basin or mould in cold water, add the jelly and leave until set.

Variations: Jelly Cream: use slightly less water than given above, i.e. ½ pint (300 ml) only if using fruit squash(but ¾ pint (450 ml) if using a jelly tablet). Allow the jelly to stiffen slightly then add a good ¼ pint (150 ml) whipped evaporated milk (see page 39).

.Milk Jelly: soften then dissolve ½ oz (15 g) gelatine in 4 tablespoons water; when cold add 1 pint (600 ml) less 4 tablespoons milk and a little flavouring essence. Make a fruit-flavoured jelly; when cold and beginning to stiffen whisk in 3 tablespoons dried milk powder.

Egg Custard

Reconstitute 2 dried eggs. Beat with 1 oz (25 g) sugar until smooth. Add ½ pint (300 ml) milk for a thick custard or ¾-1 pint (450-600 ml) milk for a thinner custard. Cook over hot water, whisking all the time until smooth and thickened. Add a little vanilla essence to flavour.

To Whip Evaporated Milk

METHOD 1. Put the can of milk into a saucepan then add enough water to cover it. Boil the water briskly for 15 minutes. Check it covers the can throughout this time. Allow the can of milk to cool, open it and whisk it.

METHOD 2. To give a stiffer texture: boil the can of milk in water. At the end of 15 minutes open it carefully, protecting your hands, as it may spurt out. Pour the hot milk into a bowl. Soften 1 teaspoon gelatine in 2 tablespoons cold water then add to the very hot evaporated milk and blend thoroughly. Chill the mixture for several hours, or even overnight, then whisk briskly.

Mock Creams

Blend 1 tablespoon cornflour, arrowroot or custard powder (whichever is available) with ¼ pint (150 ml) milk. Pour into a saucepan and stir over a low heat until thickened. Allow to become absolutely cold.

Cream 1 oz (25 g) butter or margarine with 1 oz (25 g) sugar (icing sugar is best, if available). Very gradually beat teaspoons at a time of the thickened cornflour and milk mixture into the creamed fat and sugar. The more it is beaten the lighter it becomes. For a thin cream use just 1 teaspoon cornflour ,or arrowroot or custard powder.

Recipe 2: Soften 2 teaspoons gelatine in 2 tablespoons cold water then dissolve over a pan of very hot water. Allow to become quite cold, but not set.

Cream 2 oz (50 g) butter or margarine and 2 oz (50 g) sugar (icing sugar, if possible). Gradually beat the cold gelatine into the creamed ingredients.

For a thinner cream gradually add 2 tablespoons milk after the gelatine has been incorporated.

Mock Lemon Curd

Blend 1 teaspoon cornflour with 4 tablespoons lemon squash and 3 tablespoons water. Pour into a saucepan, add 1 oz (25 g) margarine, 1 oz (25 g) sugar and a pinch of citric or tartaric acid. Stir over a low heat until the mixture thickens and becomes clear. This should take about 10 minutes. Remove the curd from the heat. Stir the mixture as it cools to prevent a skin forming.

Home-made Ice Cream

PREPARATION TIME: 20 MINUTES PLUS FREEZING TIME

COOKING TIME: 15 MINUTES FOR MAKING THE CUSTARD AND BOILING THE EVAPORATED MILK.

QUANTITY: 6 HELPINGS

½ pint (300 ml) custard (made as page 38 or with custard powder), sweetened to taste
1 can evaporated milk, whipped (see above)
flavouring (see method)

Blend together the cold custard and the whipped evaporated milk. Add a flavouring (see below) and put into the freezing compartment of a refrigerator set at its coldest position; freeze until 'mushy'. Take out, beat hard then return to the freezing compartment to continue freezing.

Flavourings: Chocolate: blend 1-1½ tablespoons sifted cocoa powder into the hot custard. Add a few drops of vanilla essence, too.

Coffee: add 1-2 tablespoons coffee essence to hot custard or make the custard with part milk and part liquid coffee.

Fruit: omit custard and add ¼-½ pint (150-300 ml) thick sweetened fruit purée to the whipped evaporated cream.

Vanilla: add 1 teaspoon vanilla essence to hot custard.

V
V

CHILDREN'S CELEBRATIONS

Children were very fortunate during the Victory celebrations, for they often attended many parties, including street parties, family parties and special children's events at school or in their own homes. In some cases children had remained evacuated to safer areas, so they, like members of the Forces, were returning home. Sometimes parties were made more elaborate by encouraging the children to go in fancy dress.

The menus for these parties would be mostly sweet foods, cakes and biscuits, with sausage rolls, or other simple savouries, and there would be sandwiches of various kinds. You will find typical recipes of the period for all these in this chapter.

Among the most usual desserts for children were jelly (made as page 38) and blancmange. Blancmange powders were available but, as the years went by, they tended to have very synthetic flavours. If fresh milk was scarce the blancmange would be made either with diluted evaporated or condensed milk (both sold on points) or with the powdered Household milk.

..Shoot straight, Lady

MAKING PASTRY

It was very difficult to make good pastry during the war years, for not only was fat scarce but the flour became much heavier in texture. Some of the ways in which cooks compensated for the lack of fat are given here. Cooks who had used plain flour for pastry, now often chose self-raising flour to give a lighter texture.

SHORTCRUST PASTRY

PREPARATION TIME: 10 MINUTES

COOKING TIME: AS IN THE RECIPES

QUANTITY: DEPENDS UPON THE RECIPE

8 oz (225 g) plain or self-raising flour
pinch salt
4 oz (110 g*) fat - margarine and lard mixed or cooking fat or good dripping
cold water to bind
*** use this metrication to give the classic proportions of half fat to flour**

Sift the flour and salt into a mixing bowl. Rub in the fat until the mixture is like fine breadcrumbs. Add sufficient water to make a dough with a firm rolling consistency.

Variations: These low-fat pastries were best eaten hot.

Low-fat Shortcrust: use self-raising flour and 2 oz (50 g) fat. Bind with milk instead of water, if possible, to add a little more fat to the mixture.

Oatmeal Shortcrust: omit 2 oz (50 g) flour and add 2 oz (50 g) fine oatmeal or rolled oats instead. This is very good when using only 2 oz (50 g) fat. Bind with water or milk to make a pleasantly 'nutty' flavoured pastry.

Potato Shortcrust: rub 2 oz (50 g) fat into 4 oz (110 g) flour and a good pinch of salt. Add 4 oz (110 g*) very smooth potato, mashed without any extra liquid or fat. Mix well, then add cold water or milk to make a firm rolling consistency. Very little liquid should be required.*

SAUSAGE ROLLS

PREPARATION TIME: 20 MINUTES

COOKING TIME: SEE METHOD

QUANTITY: 6-14

In pre-war days flaky pastry would have been used to make these rolls but in 1945 this had become a memory, for it required such a high proportion of fat.

Shortcrust Pastry made with 8 oz (225 g) flour, etc (see recipe above)
8 oz (225 g) sausagemeat
little milk, to glaze

Preheat the oven to 200°C (400°F), Gas Mark 6. The Shortcrust Pastry makes excellent sausage rolls, as do the variations and the American Baking Powder Pastry on page 43, if you can serve the rolls hot or warm. The more economical pastries tend to become rather hard when cold.

Roll out the pastry and cut into two strips, about 5 inches (13 cm) wide and 14 inches (35.5 cm) long. Moisten the sides of the pastry with a little water.

Place the sausagemeat in the centre of each strip. Fold the pastry to enclose this and seal the edges firmly.

For small sausage rolls cut each strip into 6-7 portions, for larger ones into 3-4 portions only. Make 2 slits on top of each roll and brush with milk. Put on to a baking sheet. Bake in a preheated oven, allowing the small rolls 20 minutes and the larger ones 25-28 minutes.

Variation: If sausagemeat is scarce blend each 6 oz (175 g) with 2 oz (50 g) seasoned mashed potato.

AMERICAN BAKING POWDER PASTRY

PREPARATION TIME: 15 MINUTES

COOKING TIME: AS SPECIFIC RECIPES

QUANTITY: AS SPECIFIC RECIPES

This is a very low fat pastry which must be eaten as soon as possible after baking.

8 oz (225 g) self-raising flour with 1 teaspoon baking powder or plain flour with 3 teaspoons baking powder
pinch salt
1-2 oz (25-50 g) margarine or cooking fat
1 tablespoon sugar, for sweet dishes
water to bind

Sift the flour and baking powder with the salt, rub in the margarine or cooking fat until the mixture is like fine breadcrumbs. Add the sugar if required. Gradually blend in sufficient cold water to make a rolling consistency. Bake the pastry as soon as possible.

USING AMERICAN BAKING POWDER PASTRY

These dishes use the amount of pastry given on this page.

SAVOURY DISHES

Sardine Fingers: roll out the pastry as thinly as possible, cut into two oblong pieces. Mash 2 large cans of sardines in tomato sauce (obtainable on points). Spread over the bottom piece of pastry and top with the other piece. Bake in a preheated oven, 200°C (400°F), Gas Mark 6, for about 25 minutes, or until firm, then cut into 24 fingers.

Cheese and Carrot Fingers: follow the recipe above but blend 4 oz (100 g) grated cheese with 4 oz (100 g) grated raw carrots and a very little mayonnaise (page 17) or milk. Use as the filling and bake as above.

Beef and Tomato Fingers: follow the recipe above but mash 8 oz (225 g) corned beef with 2 skinned and chopped tomatoes (or use 2-3 tablespoons tomato ketchup instead). Use as the filling and bake as above.

SWEET DISHES

Apple Fingers: follow the recipe above but use thick apple pulp, sweetened with honey plus 2-3 tablespoons chopped dates, as the filling. Bake as above.

Jam or Marmalade Fingers: use jam or marmalade as the filling. Dust the cooked slices with sifted icing sugar.

CHOUX BUNS

PREPARATION TIME: 10 MINUTES

COOKING TIME: 25-30 MINUTES

QUANTITY: 12-15

Choux pastry was regarded as a pre-war luxury until people realised it could be made with dried eggs. For special occasions, Mock Cream or fruit fillings would be used.

¼ pint (150 ml) water
1-2 oz (25-50 g) margarine
1 teaspoon sugar
2½ oz (65 g) plain flour
pinch salt
2 reconstituted dried or fresh eggs
Mock Cream (page 39), to fill
Chocolate Icing (page 47), for topping

Preheat the oven to 200°C (400°F), Gas Mark 6. Grease 2 baking trays.

Put the water and margarine into a saucepan, heat until the margarine has melted, remove from the heat.

Sift the flour and salt and add to the pan. Stir briskly to blend then return to a very low heat and stir until the mixture forms a ball and leaves the inside of the saucepan quite clean around the base and sides. This stage is important.

Allow the mixture to cool thoroughly. Beat the eggs well and gradually beat into the flour mixture; you may not need quite all of the second egg, for the mixture should have a sticky consistency.

Put 12-15 heaps of the pastry on the trays and bake for 25-30 minutes until well-risen, golden and quite firm. Cool away from a draught. Split the buns, if there is any slightly uncooked mixture inside remove it.

When quite cold fill with Mock Cream and top with the Chocolate Icing.

Variations: Top the buns with sifted icing sugar, if available, instead of Chocolate Icing.

Eclairs: make finger shapes instead of heaps on the trays. Bake for about 20-25 minutes.

BABY DOUGHNUTS

PREPARATION TIME: 10 MINUTES

COOKING TIME: 6-7 MINUTES FOR EACH BATCH

QUANTITY: ABOUT 18 SMALL DOUGHNUTS

These are really rather like thick fritters, but children enjoyed their sugary taste.

8 oz (225 g) self-raising flour or plain flour sifted with 2 teaspoons baking powder
1 reconstituted dried or fresh egg
1 oz (25 g) margarine, melted
1 oz (25 g) sugar
¼ pint (150 ml) milk or milk and water
2 oz (50 g) cooking fat or dripping, for frying
1½ oz (40 g) sugar, to coat

Sift the flour, or flour and baking powder, into a bowl. Add the other ingredients, except the fat and sugar, and blend well until a very thick smooth batter.

Heat half the cooking fat or dripping in a frying pan, add about 9 small spoonfuls of the batter, cook steadily for 3-3½ minutes then turn over and cook for the same time on the second side. To test if cooked press firmly with the back of a knife, the doughnuts should feel firm.

Lift the doughnuts out of the pan, cool and then roll in some of the sugar.

Repeat this process with the rest of the batter, fat and sugar.

WHISKED SPONGE SLAB

PREPARATION TIME: 15 MINUTES

COOKING TIME: 12-15 MINUTES

QUANTITY: 1 CAKE

This is an ideal sponge to bake as a large fairly flat cake, that can be cut up into small squares to make decorated cakes for small children.

If eggs are not available, see the Eggless 'Sponge' below. While dried eggs did not make as good a sponge as fresh eggs, the result was very palatable.

3 oz (85 g*) self-raising flour or plain flour sifted with 1 teaspoon baking powder**
3 reconstituted dried or fresh eggs
4 oz (110 g*) sugar, use caster if possible
*** use this metrication**
**** This generous amount of baking powder was because of the heavy wartime flour; reduce this to ¾ teaspoon with today's flour.**

Preheat the oven to 190°C (375°F), Gas Mark 5. Line a Swiss Roll tin, about 12 x 8-9 inches (30.5 x 20-23 cm) with well-greased margarine paper or greaseproof paper, if you have any available.

Sift the flour, or flour and baking powder, and leave it in the kitchen on a plate while whisking the eggs;, this

will help to lighten the sponge.

Put the eggs and sugar into a mixing bowl and whisk hard until the mixture thickens. With dried eggs you get a better result if the bowl is placed over a pan of hot, but not boiling, water and the ingredients whisked until they thicken, then the bowl removed from the heat and the eggs and sugar whisked until cold.

Fold the flour, or flour and baking powder, into the whisked eggs and sugar. Pour into the tin and bake until firm to the touch, this takes approximately 12-15 minutes. Lift from the tin and place on a wire cooling tray.

Variations: Iced Sponge Cakes: cover the top of the sponge with Glacé Icing (page 47). Allow this to set then cut the cake into small squares.

Each cake can be topped with a small sweet to make them look pretty or the icing can be 'feathered'.

Sponge Sandwich: grease and flour two 6½-7 inch (16.5-18 cm) sandwich tins, or line them with greased margarine paper. Divide the mixture between the tins and bake for about 15 minutes. Cool for 2-3 minutes then turn out. Sandwich together with jam or jam and Mock Cream (page 39) and top with Glacé Icing.

Swiss Roll: Make and bake 1 recipe quantity of the Whisked Sponge Slab. Turn the sponge on to sugared paper, remove the cooking paper, spread with warm jam and roll firmly.

EGGLESS 'SPONGE'

PREPARATION TIME: 10 MINUTES

COOKING TIME: 15 MINUTES

QUANTITY: MAKES 1 CAKE

Eggless recipes were very much in demand. Although this is not a true sponge the flavour is very acceptable. It can be used in the same way as the Whisked Sponge Slab recipe and variations above.

3 oz (85 g*) margarine
4 oz (110 g*) sugar
1 tablespoon golden syrup
6 oz (175 g) self-raising flour sifted with 1 teaspoon baking powder or plain flour sifted with 2½ teaspoons baking powder
¼ pint (150 ml) milk or milk and water
*** use this metrication**

Preheat the oven to 190°C (375°F), Gas Mark 5. Line a Swiss Roll tin, about 12 x 8-9 inches (30.5 x 20-23 cm) with well-greased margarine paper or greaseproof paper, if you have any available.

Cream the margarine, sugar and syrup until soft and light. Fold in the sifted flour and baking powder with the milk, giving a smooth mixture.

Spoon into the tin and bake for 15 minutes or until firm to the touch.

Variation: Eggless 'Sponge' Sandwich: divide the mixture between two 6½-7 inch (16.5-18 cm) sandwich tins. Preheat the oven to 180°C (350°F), Gas Mark 4 and bake for 18-20 minutes. Cool for about 5 minutes in the tins then turn out on to a wire rack. When cold sandwich together with jam. The top can be dusted with sugar or covered with Glacé Icing (see page 47).

GLACE ICING

This is also known as Water Icing. Icing sugar could be purchased as part of the sugar ration.

Sift the sugar if it has lumps and blend with a little water. The icing can be flavoured with essence or sifted cocoa or chocolate powder or coffee essence or liquid coffee.

CHOCOLATE ICINGS

with chocolate

Melt 4 oz (100 g) plain chocolate in a basin over hot water, add ½ oz (15 g) margarine and 1 teaspoon water. Stir well then cool slightly and use as an icing.

This gives enough icing for a very thin layer in the centre of the Choux Buns.

without chocolate

Warm the syrup slightly, so you do not use too much.

Blend 2 tablespoons of warm golden syrup with 2 tablespoons sifted cocoa powder and ½ oz (15 g) melted margarine. Flavour with vanilla essence.

SPONGE BISCUITS

Preparation time: 15 minutes

Cooking time: 10-12 minutes

Quantity: 18-20 biscuits

These were ideal for very small children. They could be served plain or iced or sandwiched together with jam.

2 reconstituted dried or fresh eggs
2-3 oz (50-75 g) sugar
2½ oz (65 g) self-raising flour or plain flour sifted with ½ teaspoon baking powder
few drops vanilla essence

Preheat the oven to 200°C (400°F), Gas mark 6. Grease 2-3 baking trays well.

Put the eggs and sugar into a bowl and whisk over hot water until thick and creamy. Remove from the heat and whisk until cold. Sift the flour, or flour and baking powder. Fold into the eggs with the vanilla essence.

Feathering

Iced cakes of any kind were a treat for it was illegal for bakers to produce iced cakes. You could ice cakes at home if you had the ingredients.

Make the Glacé Icing (left). For a thick layer over the sponge slab on pages 44-5, make a double quantity.

Spread the top of the sponge with most of the icing, do not allow it to set.

Add a little sifted cocoa or a few drops of colouring to the rest of the icing and use it either to pipe lines across the cake or dip a skewer in the icing and form lines. Take the back of a knife and drag these lines towards you.

Use the knife to pull them away from you, so giving the feathered effect.

Drop small spoonfuls on to the trays, allowing plenty of space for the mixture to spread during baking.

Cook for 10-12 minutes until pale golden in colour and firm in texture. Remove from the baking trays on to a wire rack. When quite cold store in an airtight tin. They keep well for several days.

Variations: Top the biscuits with a little Glacé Icing or Chocolate Icing (left).

Sandwich pairs of biscuits together with jam.

OATY BISCUITS

Preparation time: 20 minutes

Cooking time: 15 minutes

Quantity: 24 biscuits

4 oz (115 g*) margarine or cooking fat
3 oz (85 g*) sugar
7 oz (200 g) fine oatmeal or rolled oats
5 oz (150 g) self-raising flour or plain flour sifted with 1¼ teaspoons baking powder
pinch salt
1 reconstituted dried egg or fresh egg
little milk
*** use this metrication**

Preheat the oven to 180°C (350°F), Gas Mark 4. Grease 2 baking trays well.

Cream the margarine, or cooking fat, and sugar until soft and light, add the oatmeal, or rolled oats, and mix well. Sift the flour, or flour and baking powder, with the salt, add to the oat mixture with the egg. Mix very thoroughly before adding the milk, for the drier the biscuit dough the better the biscuits.

Gradually stir in enough milk to make a firm dough. Knead the dough and roll out on a floured board until about ¼ inch (5 mm) in thickness. Cut into small shapes and put on to the baking trays. Bake for 15 minutes or until firm and golden. Cool on the baking trays.

Store in an airtight tin, away from other biscuits.

SPICED BISCUITS

PREPARATION TIME: 25 MINUTES

COOKING TIME: 10 MINUTES

QUANTITY: 30 BISCUITS

2 oz (50 g) lard or cooking fat
2 oz (50 g) sugar
1 tablespoon golden syrup
6 oz (175 g) plain flour
½ teaspoon bicarbonate of soda
pinch ground cinnamon, or to taste
pinch ground ginger, or to taste
little water

Preheat the oven to 160°C (325°F), Gas Mark 3. Grease 2 baking trays.

Cream the lard, or fat, with the sugar and syrup. Sift the flour with the bicarbonate of soda and spices. Add to the creamed ingredients. Mix very well and then add just enough water to make a firm dough. Turn out on to a lightly floured board, roll out until just ¼ inch (5 mm) in thickness. Cut into 30 rounds. Place on the baking trays and bake 10 minutes.

Cool the biscuits on the baking trays.

Crumb Sponge

As nuts were unavailable this way of using crisp breadcrumbs was sometimes recommended for making a 'nutty' textured sponge. Use the same ingredients as for the Whisked Sponge Slab on page 44 but substitute 3 oz (85 g) crisp fine breadcrumbs for the flour.*

The mixture does not rise as well but it does give an interesting texture. You can fold 1 small teaspoon baking powder into the whisked eggs and sugar before adding the crumbs to make a lighter texture. Flavour the mixture with a few drops of almond essence.

** use this metrication*

CARROT BUNS

PREPARATION TIME: 15 MINUTES

COOKING TIME: 12-15 MINUTES

QUANTITY: 12 BUNS

It is important that the carrots are freshly grated and not put into water before use

8 oz (225 g) self-raising flour or plain flour sifted with 2 teaspoons baking powder
3 oz (75 g) margarine or cooking fat
3 oz (75 g) sugar
4 tablespoons finely grated raw carrot
2 tablespoons sultanas (optional)
1 reconstituted dried or fresh egg
little milk or water

Preheat the oven to 220°C (425°F), Gas Mark 7. Grease 2 baking trays.

Sift the flour, or flour and baking powder, into a mixing bowl, rub in the margarine or cooking fat, add the sugar, carrots, sultanas and egg. Mix well then add sufficient milk or water to make a sticky consistency.

Put 12 small heaps on the baking trays and cook for 12-15 minutes or until firm and golden in colour.

PATRIOTIC PUDDING

PREPARATION TIME: 20 MINUTES

COOKING TIME: 1½ HOURS

QUANTITY: 4-6 HELPINGS

This well known steamed pudding appeared first in the recommendations for feeding children at school dinners in a Board of Education booklet in 1939.

8 oz (225 g) self-raising flour or plain flour sifted with 2 teaspoons baking powder
pinch salt
3-4 oz (75-100 g) margarine or cooking fat
3 oz (75 g) sugar
1 egg, beaten
milk and water to mix
3-4 tablespoons golden syrup, jam, lemon curd or marmalade

Sift the flour, or flour and baking powder, with the salt into a mixing bowl. Rub in the margarine or fat, add the sugar, the egg and enough milk and water to make a soft dropping consistency (like thick whipped cream). Put the syrup or other ingredients, then the pudding mixture into a well greased 1-1½ pint (600-900 ml) basin, cover with margarine paper or greased greaseproof paper and steam over rapidly boiling water for 40 minutes then lower the heat and continue steaming for a further 50 minutes. Turn out and serve with custard.

Variations: In 1939, when the Board of Education Booklet was prepared, dried eggs were not available. A reconstituted dried egg could be used instead of a fresh egg.

For a lighter pudding increase the eggs to 2. Instead of the syrup or jam or curd or marmalade put soaked, but not cooked, dried prunes or figs in the basin or use peeled, cored and sliced cooking apples.

Add 3-4 oz (75-100 g) raisins or sultanas or chopped dates to the flour mixture before mixing with the egg and milk and water.

JELLIED TRIFLE

PREPARATION TIME: 10 MINUTES

NO COOKING

QUANTITY: 4-6 HELPINGS

This was another favourite pudding with children at their school dinners. It would not have been served on either VE or VJ Days for schools were closed in celebration of the former day and on their annual summer holiday in August. It may well have been served in the days that followed these historic events. It appealed to children who did not like custard, for although it was served with custard this could be refused if desired.

1 pint (600 ml) jelly (see page 38)
4-6 oz (100-175 g) stale plain cake
4-6 oz (100-175 g) fresh fruit such as dessert apples or plums or soft fruit or 3-4 oz (75-100 g) dried fruit, such as cooked prunes or apple rings or stoned dates

Make the jelly, as page 38, and allow it to become cold. Crumble the cake into small pieces. Dice or slice the fruit, if necessary. Add the crumbled cake and the prepared fruit to the jelly. Spoon into a bowl or individual dishes and leave until set. The trifle may be served with cold custard, if liked.

L.C.C.
W.V.S.

VOLUNTARY SERVICES CELEBRATIONS

The many thousands of people who volunteered to help the war effort by taking on service work, often in addition to their everyday work had every right to celebrate in grand style, for their work had not only been invaluable, but was unremitting. Many of them had regularly risked their lives during and after air raids in towns and cities throughout Britain.

For the ARP services, the Women's Institute, with its branches all over the country, the WVS and the many groups of essential workers, including ambulance drivers and fire brigade crews, as well as the many more I have not been able to mention in this chapter, VE and VJ Days were wonderful reasons for celebration.

THE ARP SERVICE

ARP (Air Raid Precaution Service) volunteers were on duty before, and during, air raids. They often had to rescue people from bombed buildings and this was done without thought of their own lives.

Many old and young people who worked hard all day did duty at night-time as fire watchers. Their job was very important because they were the people who would spot the first fires and give immediate warning. Harrods store in London, for instance, had its own ARP organisation, totalling 700 people, including Control Officers, Senior Pickets, Permanent Pickets, Wardens, Fireguards, Women's Civil Defence Services, Harrods Firemen and Auxiliary Firemen, Special Police and other staff.

The following recipes, from a booklet issued by the WVS on Communal Feeding in War Time, were the kinds of food offered to ARP workers at centres and canteens established in all large towns to give people hot drinks, food and a welcome brief period of leisure.

QUICK SNACKS

These were the kind of 'easy-to-eat' snacks weary ARP workers would have snatched in a brief respite from duty. Hot drinks, especially tea, cocoa or coffee, were often their greatest need.

CHEESE DREAMS

Make one or two sandwiches of bread, margarine and grated, or sliced, cheese. A little chutney could be included, if available. Dip the sandwiches in a beaten reconstituted dried or fresh egg mixed with 1-2 tablespoons milk, and fry in hot cooking fat until crisp and golden brown. Serve with salad.

CHEESE POTATOES

Bake large potatoes and split into halves. Scoop out the centre pulp, mix with grated cheese and seasoning. Return to the potato skins. Reheat and serve.

CHEESE PUDDING

PREPARATION TIME: 10 MINUTES
COOKING TIME: 30 MINUTES
QUANTITY: 3-4 HELPINGS

½ pint (300 ml) milk
1 oz (25 g) margarine
2 oz (50 g) soft breadcrumbs
1 reconstituted dried or fresh egg
3 oz (75 g) cheese, grated
salt and pepper

Pour the milk into a saucepan, add the margarine and heat until the margarine melts. Remove from the heat; add the breadcrumbs and allow to stand for 15 minutes.

Whisk the egg and add to the breadcrumb mixture with the cheese and seasoning. Mix well.

Preheat the oven to 190°C (375°F), Gas Mark 5. Pour the cheese mixture into a greased 6-7 inch (15-18 cm) soufflé dish or 1 pint (600 ml) pie dish. Bake for 30 minutes or until well-risen and golden brown. Serve at once with a green vegetable.

BEANS ON TOAST

Heat canned beans and serve on hot toast. They can be topped with a fried egg.

TOMATOES ON TOAST

Halve, season and fry tomatoes, put on to hot toast and top with grilled or fried sausages.

HERB OMELETTE

Beat 2 reconstituted dried or fresh eggs. Season and add about 1 tablespoon chopped mixed herbs or 1 teaspoon dried herbs.

Heat 1 oz (25g) margarine or cooking fat in a pan. Add the egg mixture and cook until set at the bottom then tilt the pan so the top liquid egg runs underneath and continue cooking until set.

Fold, away from the handle, and serve. The omelette could be filled with crisp chopped bacon or grated cheese or cooked tomatoes.

Spanish Omelette

Dice 2 cooked potatoes, finely chop a small onion, heat 1 oz (25 g) margarine and heat the vegetables. Add the seasoned eggs and cook until firm. Do not fold.

IN THE COUNTRY

The Women's Institute members were a very important group, for they tackled various wartime jobs in the countryside and played a vital role in village life. They helped with agricultural work, and the preserves they made for Britain with local fruit became part of the official jam ration. In many cases, they were related to farmers or farm workers and cooked for the Land Army workers and the farmers. A typical selection of country dishes have been included in the chapter on Country Celebrations.

ESSENTIAL WORKERS

Ambulance crews and the Fire Brigade members worked both night and day to deal with the many accidents caused by the war, as well as carrying out their everyday commitments.

THE WVS

The WVS (Women's Voluntary Service) was created just before the war, and its members did an enormous range of jobs during the war. A book entitled 'The Story of the WVS', sadly now out of print, gives a very clear picture of their work and importance during, and after, the war.

The service, always known as the WVS, was formed in 1938. When it became apparent that there was going to be a war in the foreseeable future, the Dowager Lady Reading approached the then Home Secretary, Sir Samuel Hoare, with a view to recruiting women to help in work connected with Air Raid Precautions. Sir Samuel wanted a force of a million standing by.

It says much for Lady Reading's remarkable gift for leadership and for her ability to convince women that even if they only gave a few hours service a week it would make an incalculable difference to the course of events, that so many women dropped their colanders and ran. Starting with a membership of five, by the end of its first year the WVS was 300,000 strong.

Their first wartime job was to help with the evacuation of city children and mothers to safer areas. They became volunteer drivers to all departments, served endless meals at Emergency Feeding Centres after air-raids, manned canteens for Air Raid Wardens and in various Service Clubs throughout Britain. They later extended this to become partners to NAAFI in some combat zones. They even set up club rooms in Paris and Brussels after the successful D Day landings led to victory in Europe.

Post-war acknowledgement of the wonderful work done by the WVS both during the war and afterwards - and which the organisation is still doing - came in 1966, when the Queen honoured the WVS by adding 'Royal' to its title, since when the service's full name has been Women's Royal Voluntary Service.

It is certain that WVS celebrations for both VE and VJ Days would be enjoyed by an enormous number of people in Britain and in other countries where these women were doing such invaluable and cheerful work. The recipes included in this chapter come from a WVS wartime handbook of recipes and other WVS collections of recipes and cooking hints collected by local WVS groups.

Cream of Parsnip Soup

Preparation time: 25 minutes

Cooking time: 35-40 minutes

Quantity: 4-5 helpings

This is particularly good in summertime when parsnips are young, sweet in flavour and very tender.

1 lb (450 g) parsnips, peeled and minced or grated
4 oz (100 g) onions or leeks, finely chopped
2 bacon rinds
2 pints (1.2 litres) stock or water
salt and pepper
1 oz (25 g) flour
¼ pint (150 ml) milk
chopped parsley, to garnish

Put the parsnips, onions or leeks and bacon rinds into a saucepan with the stock or water. Bring to the boil, season to taste, cover the pan and boil steadily until the vegetables are tender. Blend the flour gradually with the milk, add to the soup, stirring well to prevent any lumps forming. Remove the bacon rinds, add any extra seasoning required. Garnish with the parsley.

Tomato Soup

Preparation time: 20 minutes

Cooking time: 30-35 minutes

Quantity: 4-5 helpings

One of the many tasks undertaken by the WVS was to collect and supply fresh vegetables to mine sweepers and other small ships around the coasts of Britain, the crews of which had no opportunity of gathering these for themselves. WVS womenn were therefore used to finding vegetables and fruit, so for Victory celebrations would undoubtedly make this soup, which was a favourite with old and young. It was an ideal summertime soup, for fresh tomatoes would be readily available for several months.

¾ oz (20 g) dripping
1 small carrot, sliced
1 small potato, sliced
1 small onion, sliced
2 bacon rinds
2½ pints (1.5 litres) stock or water
12 oz (350 g) tomatoes, halved
salt and pepper
2 oz (50 g) flour
1 teaspoon sugar

Heat the dripping in a saucepan and fry the carrot, potato, onion and bacon rinds for a few minutes. Boil most of the stock or water, add to the ingredients in the saucepan with the tomatoes and a little seasoning. Cover the pan and boil gently until the vegetables are tender. Mash with a wooden spoon or put through a sieve. Return to the saucepan. Blend the flour with the rest of the stock or water, which should be cold. Add to the pan and stir over the heat until thickened. Adjust the seasoning and add the sugar.

Cod and Tomato Fish Cakes

Preparation time: 25 minutes

Cooking time: 25-30 minutes

Quantity: 4-5 helpings

The good amounts of tomato, onion and parsley help to make up for the rather small proportion of fish in these fish cakes.

½ oz (15 g) cooking fat
1 small onion, finely chopped
1 large tomato, finely chopped
1½ lb (675 g) cooked potatoes, mashed
8 oz (225 g) cooked fish, flaked
salt and pepper
1 tablespoon chopped parsley
2 oz (50 g) crisp breadcrumbs, to coat

THE SPHERE [AUGUST 1, 1942

DIG FOR VICTORY

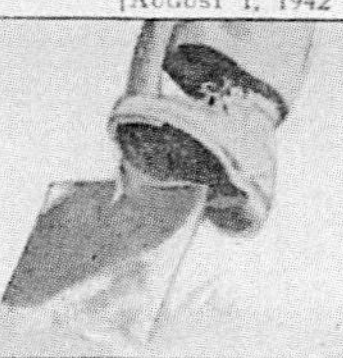

G.E.1095

GUINNESS for STRENGTH

Heat the fat and add the onion and tomato, cook until a soft purée. Blend with the mashed potatoes, fish, seasoning and parsley. Form into 8-10 round cakes. Coat in the crisp breadcrumbs.

Preheat the oven to 190°C (375°F), Gas Mark 5. Grease and heat a baking tray. Put the fish cakes on this and bake for 15-20 minutes, or until crisp and brown.

Variation: Fry the cakes in hot fat, if available.

For a better coating, dust the fish cakes with seasoned flour, brush with beaten egg and coat in the crumbs. When more fish is available use only 12 oz (350 g) mashed potato and the same weight of cooked fish.

Salmon Loaf

Preparation time: 25 minutes

Cooking time: 1 hour

Quantity: 4-5 helpings

6 oz (175 g) canned pink salmon
nearly ¼ pint (150 ml) milk (see method)
3 oz (75 g) stale bread
4 tablespoons cold water
½ oz (15 g) margarine, melted
3 oz (75 g) cooked potatoes, mashed
½ tablespoon chopped parsley
salt and pepper
½ tablespoon vinegar

Open the can of fish and pour the liquid into a measure, add enough milk to make ¼ pint (150 ml). Break the bread into small pieces, put into a basin, add the water, soak for about 15 minutes, then squeeze dry.

Flake the salmon, then mix all the ingredients together, put into a greased 1 lb (450 g) loaf tin or oblong casserole. Cover with greased greaseproof paper. Preheat the oven to 180°C (350°F), Gas Mark 4. Bake for 1 hour. Serve hot or cold.

Variation: The loaf can be steamed for 1 hour instead of being baked.

Cornish Pasties

Preparation time: 30 minutes

Cooking time: 30 minutes

Quantity: 4-5 helpings

In the original WVS recipe for these favourites, there are hints on making the pasties quickly, not individually, but as the recipe has been adapted for a small number of helpings it now allows for making the more traditional individual pasties.

Shortcrust Pastry made with
1 lb (450 g) flour etc. (page 42)
For the filling:
4 oz (100 g) minced beef
1 medium onion, finely chopped
8 oz (225 g) turnips, finely diced
2 oz (50 g) carrots, finely diced
little stock
salt and pepper
little milk, to glaze

Preheat the oven to 190°C (375°F), Gas Mark 5. Make the pastry as on page 42, roll out and cut into 4 or 5 large rounds.

Mix the ingredients for the filling together, moisten with a very little stock and season to taste. Put spoonfuls of the filling into the centre of each pastry round. Brush the edges of the pastry with water, bring these together and flute them to make the traditional pastie shape. Brush with a little milk.

Put the pasties on a greased baking sheet and bake in the preheated oven for 30 minutes.

Variations: Use one of the alternative kinds of pastry on pages 23 and 43 instead of Shortcrust Pastry.

When more meat is available use 8 oz (225 g) minced beef, 8 oz (225 g) finely diced potato with 2 chopped onions and omit the other vegetables.

Raised Pork Pie

Preparation time: 40 minutes

Cooking time: 2 hours

Quantity: 8-10 helpings

For the pastry:

1 lb (450 g) plain flour

1 teaspoon salt

4 oz (100 g) cooking fat or well clarified dripping (see below)

½ pint (300 ml) water

For the filling:

1 lb (450 g) pork sausage meat

6 oz (175 g) fat bacon, minced

2 medium onions, finely chopped

1 tablespoon chopped mixed herbs or ½ teaspoon dried mixed herbs

salt and pepper

To glaze:

1 reconstituted dried or fresh egg

1 tablespoon water

Sift the flour and salt into a mixing bowl, keep in a warm place. Put the cooking fat or dripping into a saucepan with the water. Heat until the fat or dripping has melted. Pour on to the flour and mix well. Keep warm until using this.

Blend all the ingredients for the filling together.

Knead the pastry until a smooth pliable paste. Roll out two-thirds and line the base and sides of a 7-8 inch (18-20 cm) cake tin, preferably one with a loose base. Put in the filling. Damp the edges of the pastry. Roll out the remaining dough to make a lid, press in position.

Make a slit in the centre of the pastry covering, for the steam to escape during baking. Any pastry left can be made into leaf shapes to decorate the pastry. Beat the egg with the water and brush over the pastry.

Preheat the oven to 180°C (350°F), Gas Mark 4 and bake the pie for 2 hours. Serve cold with salad.

Variation: If fresh pork is available use half finely diced lean pork and half sausage meat.

Clarifying Dripping

Put the dripping in a saucepan with cold water to cover. Bring gradually to the boil, removing any scum. Strain into a bowl and cool. When cold, carefully lift off the fat which has set on top of the water and scrape the bottom. Heat the fat gently in a saucepan until all the water in it has evaporated. The clarified fat is now ready for use for frying or baking.

WVS Special Sandwich Fillings

Watercress and Salmon

Blend the boned salmon from a small can with 1-2 tablespoons vinegar, 4 oz (100 g) chopped watercress, 6 oz (175 g) mashed potatoes, 4 oz (100 g) finely chopped leek and salt and pepper to taste.

Savoury Egg and Bacon

Heat 1 oz (25 g) margarine in a pan, add 2 oz (50 g) chopped spring onions, 2 oz (50 g) finely chopped cooked bacon, and heat for a few minutes. Reconstitute 4 dried eggs or use fresh eggs, beat with 6 tablespoons milk, pour into the pan, add a little salt and pepper and cook gently until the eggs have set, stirring occasionally. Allow to become cold.

Pilchard and Leek Spread

Blend 8 oz (225 g) canned pilchards in tomato sauce with 2 oz (50 g) finely chopped leeks, 2 oz (50 g) chopped parsley, 8 oz (225 g) mashed potatoes, 1 tablespoon vinegar and salt and pepper to taste.

Rhubarb Snow

Preparation time: 20 minutes

Cooking time: 20 minutes

Quantity: 4-5 helpings

Golden syrup was one of the most valuable wartime commodities and was often used in place of sugar. It was included on the points system.

12 oz (350 g) rhubarb
1-2 tablespoons water
3 oz (75 g) golden syrup
½ pint (300 ml) milk
1½ oz (40 g) semolina
few drops lemon essence

Cut the rhubarb into small pieces, put into a saucepan. Add the water (use 2 tablespoons if rhubarb is not very ripe) and the syrup. Cook until a thick pulp.

Pour the milk into a second saucepan, whisk on the semolina, add the lemon essence. Bring to the boil, then stir over a low heat for 10 minutes. Allow to cool for a few minutes then tip into a bowl. Add the rhubarb pulp. Leave until cool but not set and beat vigorously until a frothy mixture. Spoon into a serving bowl.

Variations: When both sugar and syrup are scarce cook the fruit with just the water then add crushed saccharine tablets to the hot cooked fruit.

Summer Pudding

Preparation time: 20 minutes

Cooking time: 10 minutes

Quantity: 4-5 helpings

1½ lb (675 g) soft fruit, a mixture of red and black currants or other summer fruits
3-4 tablespoons water
sugar or golden syrup, to sweeten
8-10 oz (225-300 g) stale bread

Put the prepared fruit into a saucepan with the water (use the 4 tablespoons of water if the fruit is very firm) and sugar or syrup to sweeten. Cook only until the fruit is soft, do not allow it to become a pulp.

Cut the bread into thin slices and line a 1-1½ pint (600-900 ml) basin with most of this (save enough for the top covering). Fill with the fruit and some of the juice. Cover with the remaining bread.

Put a plate and light weight on top of the pudding and leave to stand for about 12 hours. Turn the pudding out carefully and serve with the remaining juice and custard (page 38).

Apple and Date Slice

Preparation time: 25 minutes

Cooking time: 30-35 minutes

Quantity: 8-10 helpings

This was the nearest one could get to flaky pastry with rather less fat than the classic recipe and the somewhat heavier flour of the 1940s.

For the pastry:
1 lb (450 g) self-raising flour or plain flour sifted with 2 teaspoons baking powder
½ teaspoon salt
8 oz (225 g) cooking fat or margarine
water, to bind
For the filling:
1 lb (450 g) cooking apples, peeled, cored and minced or grated
8 oz (225 g) breadcrumbs
8 oz (225 g) cooking dates, minced or finely chopped
1-2 teaspoons mixed spice
2 oz (50 g) margarine or cooking fat, melted
To glaze:
1 reconstituted dried or fresh egg
1 tablespoon water

Sift the flour, or flour and baking powder, and salt into a bowl. Add the fat to the flour and cut into small pieces with one or two knives. Blend with the water to make a soft pliable dough.

Put the dough on to a floured surface and roll out then fold over, as though making puff pastry, i.e. bring up the bottom third of the dough and bring down the top third. Cover lightly and stand in a cool place for 30 minutes then roll out and fold again. Give a final rolling to make a large oblong shape. Divide this into two equal pieces.

Preheat the oven to 190°C (375°F), Gas Mark 5. Put half the pastry on to a large flat baking tray.

Mix all the ingredients for the filling together. Spread over the pastry on the baking tray. Keep the filling away from the extreme edges of the pastry. Moisten the edges with the beaten egg, mixed with the water. Cover with the second oblong of pastry. Seal the edges. Brush the top with the egg and water. Bake in the preheated oven for 30-35 minutes or until the pastry is golden brown. Cut into fingers and serve hot or cold.

Variations: When fat is scarce use the economical pastry recipe on page 43. You will need a total weight of pastry of 1½ lb (675 g).

Eggless Chocolate Buns

Preparation time: 15 minutes

Cooking time: 15-20 minutes

Quantity: 12-15 minutes

8 oz (225 g) self-raising flour or plain flour sifted with 2 teaspoons baking powder
1 oz (25 g) cocoa powder
3 oz (75 g) sugar
7½ fl oz (225 ml) hot water
1 tablespoon golden syrup
1 teaspoon bicarbonate of soda
few drops vanilla essence
3 oz (75 g) margarine, melted

Preheat the oven to 180°C (350°F), Gas Mark 4. Grease 12-15 patty tins. Sift the flour, or flour and baking powder, with the cocoa, add the sugar.

Pour the hot water into a good-sized container, add the syrup and bicarbonate of soda. This fizzes and makes the liquid rise rapidly. Add to the cocoa mixture with the essence and margarine.

Spoon into the tins and bake for 15-20 minutes or until firm to the touch. Remove from the tins on to a wire cooling rack.

Raisin and Spice Buns

Preparation time: 10 minutes

Cooking time: 15 minutes

Quantity: 12 buns

In these quickly made cakes the dried egg powder was generally added to the flour. It was however essential to add the 2 tablespoons water to the mixture before adding any extra milk or water.

8 oz (225 g) self-raising flour or plain flour sifted with 2 teaspoons baking powder
1 tablespoon dried egg powder
1 teaspoon mixed spice
2 oz (50 g) margarine or cooking fat
3 oz (75 g) sugar
3-4 oz (75-100 g) raisins
2 tablespoons water
milk or milk and water to bind

Preheat the oven to 220°C (425°F), Gas Mark 7. Grease 2 flat baking trays.

Sift the flour, or flour and baking powder, with the dried egg and spice. Rub in the margarine or cooking fat, add the sugar, raisins, water and enough milk or milk and water to make a sticky dough. It should stand in soft peaks when a knife is pulled through the mixture in the bowl.

Put spoonfuls on to the prepared trays and bake for

15 minutes, or until golden brown and firm. Remove on to a wire cooling tray.

Variation: Oaty Raisin and Spice Buns: omit 2 oz (50 g) flour and use 2 oz (50 g) rolled oats instead. Sift ½ teaspoon baking powder with the self-raising flour or still use 2 teaspoons baking powder with plain flour.

Let's talk about

HINTS FROM THE WVS

The WVS passed on in its various food booklets many practical hints, most of them based on using every last ounce of food, since nothing must be wasted in wartime. Here are some of them.

Bicarbonate of Soda in Stewed Fruit

A little bicarbonate of soda added to the fruit while stewing will neutralise some of the acid and the fruit will then need less sugar. Use ½ teaspoon bicarbonate of soda to 1 lb (450 g) fruit. Stir it in slowly at the end of the cooking time. Note, though, that this tip is not suitable for use in jam making.

Using Sardine Oil

The oil left over from a can of sardines could be utilised in the following ways:

1. Used in place of salad oil in a vinaigrette or French dressing with a fish salad.
2. Use for frying:(a) potato cakes; (b) a slice of bread to serve with potato or fish cakes; (c) fish cakes.
3. Use it for binding flaked fish and sauce for a Fish Pie.

Using Vegetable Water

The water used for cooking vegetables, which retains some of the vegetables' vitamins, should be used in the following ways:

1. For gravy, make a thick sauce and thin down with fresh vegetable water just before serving.
2. Do the same thing with soups: that is, make them fairly thick so that as the vegetables are strained, the liquor can be added to the soup to give it additional flavouring and Vitamin C.
3. When serving Cauliflower au gratin, use the liquor the cauliflower has been cooked in to make the white sauce. Use for macaroni cheese as well.

Helping the Sugar Ration Along

Stretch the sugar ration is by making full use of sweetened condensed milk and dried fruit.

Use honey and syrup, instead of sugar, to sweeten stewed fruit. Add them either before or after cooking.

Honey and syrup may also be used to replace up to half the sugar used in jam and marmalade: if your recipe needs 3 lbs (1.25 kg) sugar, you could use instead half that amount of sugar and 1½ lb (759 g) honey or syrup. Honey or syrup may be used in bottling fruit, too, but the flavour will be noticeable.

Making the MOST OF THE SUGAR

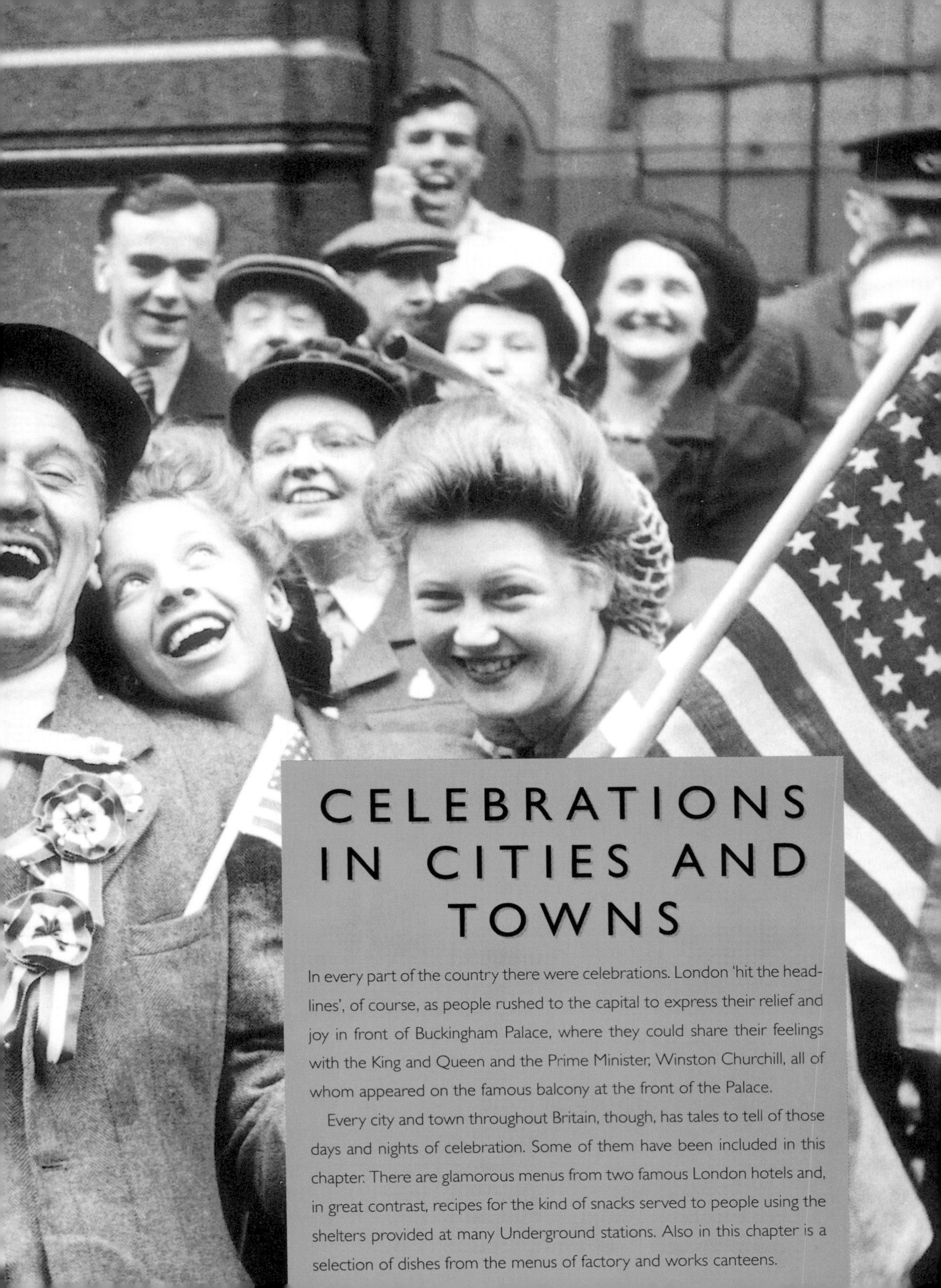

CELEBRATIONS IN CITIES AND TOWNS

In every part of the country there were celebrations. London 'hit the headlines', of course, as people rushed to the capital to express their relief and joy in front of Buckingham Palace, where they could share their feelings with the King and Queen and the Prime Minister, Winston Churchill, all of whom appeared on the famous balcony at the front of the Palace.

Every city and town throughout Britain, though, has tales to tell of those days and nights of celebration. Some of them have been included in this chapter. There are glamorous menus from two famous London hotels and, in great contrast, recipes for the kind of snacks served to people using the shelters provided at many Underground stations. Also in this chapter is a selection of dishes from the menus of factory and works canteens.

FACTORY CELEBRATIONS

Factories were situated throughout the land, of course, but most were in or on the outskirts of cities and towns, so the workers had to cope with the danger of air-raids as well as excessively hard work.

As a member of the Food Advice Division in the Ministry of Food, I had the opportunity to visit various factories and to talk to the workers during meal breaks about war-time recipes.

Factory workers, both men and women, worked incredibly hard, in day and night shifts, especially in armament and aircraft factories. Breaks in the work schedule, in the canteens or round tea trolleys on the factory floor, were cheerful interludes, usually with music as a form of relaxation.

The days following VE and VJ Days must have been full of celebration in the canteens and canteen cooks would certainly have done their best to embellish the standard menus. The recipes that follow have been selected from standard factory canteen menus, though quantities have been reduced.

Meat Pudding

PREPARATION TIME: 30 MINUTES

COOKING TIME: 2½ HOURS

QUANTITY: 4 HELPINGS

Even by the end of the war, in canteens it was not always possible to have just steak and kidney as a filling but this recipe is typical of the kind of savoury meat pudding that would be served.

For the pastry:
7 oz (200 g) plain flour, wholemeal if possible
3 oz (75 g) rolled oats or fine oatmeal
2½ teaspoons baking powder
salt and pepper
2-3 oz (50-75 g) suet, grated
water, to bind
For the filling:
8 oz (225 g) stewing steak
4 oz (100 g) liver or ox-kidney, if available (see method) or 4 oz (100 g) cooked haricot beans or cooked dried peas
4 oz (100 g) sliced onions or leeks
4 oz (100 g) sliced carrots
2 tablespoons chopped parsley

Mix the flour, oats, baking powder, seasoning and suet together then add enough cold water to make a dough with a soft rolling consistency. Roll out; use about three-quarters to line a 1½-2 pint (900-1200 ml) pudding basin. Dice the meat(s) finely; if there is no liver or ox-kidney use the beans or peas for extra protein.

Mix with the other ingredients for the filling and season well. Add 3-4 tablespoons water. Moisten the edges of the pastry then roll out the remaining dough to form a lid. Put in position, cover with margarine paper or greased greaseproof paper and steam for 2½ hours. Serve with brown gravy and mixed vegetables.

Variations: If suet is not available rub cooking fat or dripping or margarine into the flour.

Vegetable Pudding: in many homes when there was no meat left, a similar pudding would be made filled with as many different vegetables as possible.

Haricot Stew

Preparation time: 20 minutes

Cooking time: 35 minutes

Quantity: 4 servings

In canteens, just as much as in the home, fresh meat had to be augmented with corned beef and plenty of vegetables. This stew can be varied according to the vegetables in season. Leeks were used a great deal, often to take the place of onions, which were difficult to get at certain times of the year.

2 oz (50 g) dripping
1 large leek, thinly sliced
2 oz (50 g) plain flour
1½ pints (900 ml) vegetable stock
1 lb (450 g) mixed vegetables, diced
salt and pepper
4 oz (100 g) cooked haricot beans
4 oz (100 g) corned beef, diced

Heat the dripping in a large pan, add the leek and fry until brown. Blend in the flour and then the stock. Bring to the boil and cook, stirring, until thickened then add the mixed vegetables with seasoning to taste.

Cover the pan and simmer the stew until the vegetables are almost tender. Add the haricot beans and corned beef and simmer for 10 minutes to heat through.

Toad In The Hole

Preparation time: 15 minutes

Cooking time: 35-40 minutes

Quantity: 4 helpings

Canteen meals often included sausages and this was one of the favourite ways of serving them.

1 oz (25 g) dripping or cooking fat
1 lb (450 g) sausages
For the batter:
5 oz (150 g) plain flour
pinch salt
1 tablespoon dried egg powder
2 tablespoons water
½ pint (300 ml) milk or milk and water

Preheat the oven to 200°C (400°F), Gas Mark 6. Put the dripping or cooking fat into a Yorkshire Pudding tin, heat for a few minutes, add the sausages and turn around in the fat then cook for 5 minutes.

Now raise the oven setting to 220°C (425°F), Gas Mark 7. Blend the ingredients for the batter together: this is slightly less thin than for an ordinary Yorkshire Pudding batter, to make it more satisfying. (When using dried egg to make a batter, the dried egg powder was generally mixed with the flour and salt, then the water added to the liquid. This saved time.)

Pour the batter over the hot sausages and bake for 25-30 minutes, or until well risen and golden brown. Lower the heat slightly towards the end of the cooking time, if necessary.

Variations: Use a fresh egg and omit the 2 tablespoons water. Substitute Lentil sausages (recipe on page 66).

Sweet Batter Pudding: often a batter, similar to the one above, was baked and served with hot jam or golden syrup as a pudding. Use the recipe above or the more usual one of only 4 oz (110 g) flour to 1 egg and ½ pint (scant 300 ml) milk or milk and water.*

**use this metrication.*

Lentil Sausages

The following ingredients give 1 lb (450 g), or about 8 lentil sausages.

Cook 3 oz (75 g) split lentils with a chopped leek or onion, a good tablespoon of finely chopped sage and a generous amount of seasoning in water to cover until a thick soft purée.

Blend with 1 tablespoon soya or ordinary flour, a little chopped parsley and 8 oz (225 g) very smooth mashed potato. Form into sausage shapes. Coat in a beaten reconstituted dried or fresh egg and fine breadcrumbs. Fry, grill or bake until golden brown.

If using in place of ordinary sausages in Toad In The Hole (page 65) omit the coating.

Bread Pudding

PREPARATION TIME: 25 MINUTES

COOKING TIME: 1¼ HOURS

QUANTITY: 4-6 HELPINGS

A Bread Pudding is an ideal way of using up stale bread and it has always been extremely popular in this country, both as a hot pudding with custard or served cold instead of a cake. The marmalade makes up for the grated lemon and orange rinds and crystallized peel that would have been included in a good Bread Pudding in the days before the war.

8 oz (225 g) stale bread
water (see method)
2 oz (50 g) suet, shredded or margarine or cooking fat, melted
2 oz (50 g) sugar
½-1 teaspoon grated or ground nutmeg
pinch mixed spice
1-2 tablespoons marmalade
3-4 oz (75-100 g) mixed dried fruit (see method)
1 reconstituted dried or fresh egg
little milk or milk and water

Break the bread into small pieces and put into a basin, add enough cold water to cover. Leave for 30 minutes then squeeze the bread hard to extract any surplus moisture. Put the bread into a basin, add the rest of the ingredients. The dried fruit could be all of one kind or a mixture of fruits; chopped, soaked, but not cooked, dried prunes give a good flavour. Add just enough milk or milk and water to make a sticky consistency.

The pudding can be baked or steamed, if it is being served as a hot pudding, but if it is to be served cold, it is better to bake it.

If steaming, put the pudding mixture into a greased 1½-2 pint (900-1200 ml) basin. Cover with margarine paper and steam for 1½ hours.

If baking the pudding, grease a 7 inch (18 cm) cake tin. Put in the mixture. Preheat the oven to 180°C (350°F), Gas Mark 4 and bake for 1-1¼ hours, or until firm. If serving as a cake, cool in the tin then cut into squares and top with a little sugar before serving.

Apple Fruit Cake

PREPARATION TIME: 25 MINUTES

COOKING TIME: 1¼ HOURS

QUANTITY: 1 × 8 INCH (20 CM) CAKE

Teatime breaks were very important for workers in factories and cakes and buns were usually available. When apples were plentiful this was a popular cake.

12 oz (350 g) self-raising flour or plain flour sifted with 3 teaspoons baking powder
4 oz (100 g) margarine or cooking fat
4 oz (100 g) sugar
½-1 teaspoon ground cinnamon
8 oz (225 g) cooking apples, peeled, cored and diced, weight when prepared
3 oz (75 g) sultanas or raisins
1 reconstituted dried or fresh egg
milk as required
1 oz (25 g) brown sugar, for topping

Preheat the oven to 180°C (350°F), Gas Mark 4. Grease and flour an 8 inch (20 cm) cake tin.

Sift the flour, or flour and baking powder, into a mixing bowl, rub in the margarine or cooking fat, add the sugar, cinnamon, apples, sultanas or raisins and the egg. Mix very thoroughly. If necessary, add a little milk but the mixture must be a sticky consistency, i.e. it should stand up in peaks when handled with a knife.

Spoon the mixture into the cake tin, smooth flat on top and sprinkle over the brown sugar. Bake for 1¼ hours or until golden brown and firm; reduce the heat slightly after 50 minutes, if necessary. Cool for 10 minutes in the tin then turn out on to a wire cooling rack. Eat the cake when freshly baked.

CITY CELEBRATIONS

VE Day was a public holiday in Britain, so factories and shops, as well as schools, were closed. Plenty of people were working, however - like the Glasgow bus clippie waving her cap so happily in the picture on this page.

In London, where there were parades and much excitement, the world-famous Harrods department store carried out the Government's wish by opening its Food Halls and Bank, both brilliantly lighted while the rest of the store was in darkness, for several hours on VE Day morning.

Queues formed round the store from an early hour, according to the store's staff magazine, the Harrodian Gazette. 'Inside the store good spirits and tolerance were much in evidence and customers showed every co-operation,' noted the Gazette. 'Everyone was in high spirits, much shaking of hands and mutual congratulations were in evidence... It was just another of those days which none of us will ever forget.'

Despite the rationing, still very much in force of course, the store had on sale that morning fresh fish and juicy steaks and was able to provide coffee and a cold lunch for all its staff who were on duty in the store.

RESTAURANT MEALS

During and after the war food rationing brought great problems to restaurants and hotels everywhere. The leading chefs, who had been used to cooking with the best ingredients in the world, now had to make appetising and sustaining food out of limited resources. Designated First Class establishments were allowed a little leeway in catering matters and they were allowed to make a house charge.

In London at the Savoy Hotel, where the head chef was François Latry until 1942, one of the most famous dishes of the war was created by him in honour of the Minister of Food, Lord Woolton. This was, of course, Woolton Pie, for which there are many recipes; sadly, François Latry did not leave a written recipe for his original creation. My interpretation of how it might have been cooked at the Savoy starts on this page.

It is interesting to see the kinds of food served in first class hotels and restaurants during this period. The menu reproduced on page 70 comes from the famous London restaurant, Simpsons, just down The Strand from the Savoy,. and is the one they served on VE Day. Although it was a menu in celebration of a very important event, the meal's fixed price of 5s 0d (25 p), the legal maximum price for all restaurant meals, could not be increased.

The Savoy Hotel, for their official Victory In Europe Dinner on May 8th 1945, produced the following elegant menu:

The first course choice was La Tasse de Consommé Empire, or La Crème Marche Triomphale, or La Couronne de Crousacés des Vainqueurs.

This was followed by Le Poulet des Héros Alliés, with Le Velouté Champ d'Honneur and Les Feuilles de Rosée Aube de Bonheur.

For sweet, guests were offered Les Pêches Glacées de la Victoire and Les Friandises de la Paix.

The Dorchester hotel had no record of special VE Day dinners but sent me some of their wartime menus which show how imaginative their chefs had to be with sparse rations and low prices.

Welsh Rarebit

PREPARATION TIME: 15 MINUTES

COOKING TIME: 5-6 MINUTES

QUANTITY: 4 HELPINGS

This version of Welsh Rarebit was one I sampled, for it was served in the Silver Buffet restaurant at Harrods, where I so often had my lunch. It was carefully prepared, the potatoes really were beautifully smooth and the mixture was carefully seasoned to compensate for the relatively small amount of cheese used.

6 oz (175 g) cooked potatoes
1 oz (25 g) margarine, melted
4-6 oz (100-175 g) cheese, grated
little milk
salt and pepper
1 teaspoon made mustard, or to taste
few drops Worcestershire sauce
4 slices of bread

Mash the potatoes until they are absolutely smooth, blend with the margarine and three-quarters of the cheese then gradually add enough milk to make a creamy consistency. Stir in the rest of the ingredients.

Toast the bread, spread with the rarebit mixture, top with the remaining cheese and place under a preheated grill until piping hot and bubbling. Serve at once.

Woolton Pie

Most people have their own interpretation of this recipe. Basically, it is made with mixed vegetables, a sauce and a topping, which could be pastry or potatoes. I am sure the original Woolton Pie, created at the

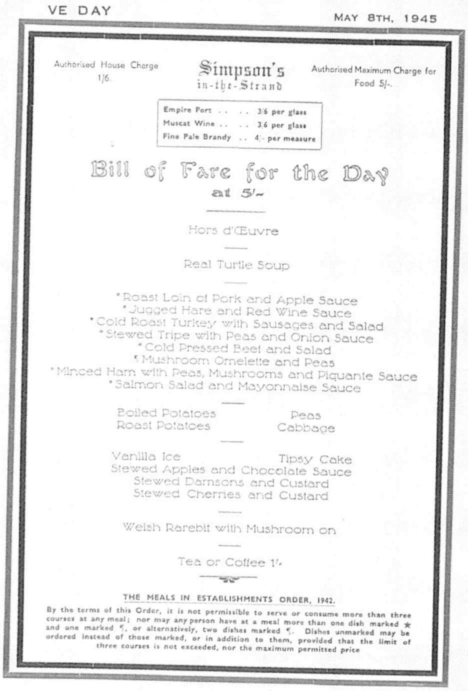

VE DAY — MAY 8TH, 1945

Authorised House Charge 1/6.

Simpson's in-the-Strand

Authorised Maximum Charge for Food 5/-.

Empire Port	3/6 per glass
Muscat Wine	3/6 per glass
Fine Pale Brandy ..	4/- per measure

Bill of Fare for the Day
at 5/-

Hors d'Œuvre

Real Turtle Soup

*Roast Loin of Pork and Apple Sauce
*Jugged Hare and Red Wine Sauce
*Cold Roast Turkey with Sausages and Salad
*Stewed Tripe with Peas and Onion Sauce
*Cold Pressed Beef and Salad
¶Mushroom Omelette and Peas
*Minced Ham with Peas, Mushrooms and Piquante Sauce
*Salmon Salad and Mayonnaise Sauce

Boiled Potatoes — Peas
Roast Potatoes — Cabbage

Vanilla Ice — Tipsy Cake
Stewed Apples and Chocolate Sauce
Stewed Damsons and Custard
Stewed Cherries and Custard

Welsh Rarebit with Mushroom on

Tea or Coffee 1/-

THE MEALS IN ESTABLISHMENTS ORDER, 1942.

By the terms of this Order, it is not permissible to serve or consume more than three courses at any meal; nor may any person have at a meal more than one dish marked ★ and one marked ¶, or alternatively, two dishes marked ¶. Dishes unmarked may be ordered instead of those marked, or in addition to them, provided that the limit of three courses is not exceeded, nor the maximum permitted price

Savoy Hotel, looked most enticing and tasted very good too.

Prepare a mixture of vegetables, such as parsnips, potatoes, leeks, carrots and any other vegetables in season. Take time and trouble to cut them into uniform shapes, such as short fingers.

Cook lightly in a little boiling water, so they retain texture and flavour. Put into a dish. Top with an interesting sauce. I imagine the Savoy might well have made a special Cheese Sauce, flavoured with herbs.

The covering might have been beautifully piped potatoes, topped with a little grated cheese, so they became brown and shining when the pie was baked for about 30 minutes in the oven.

CELEBRATIONS IN THE SHELTERS

There can be few people who celebrated the end of the war more whole-heartedly than those who had spent so much time in the air-raid shelters. Home owners throughout Britain had erected Anderson and Morrison shelters or had relatively safe places in their houses to go at the time of the air-raids.

In London there were periods when day after day, night after night, bombs fell all over the city. This is when the crowds went to the underground shelters at tube stations. No fewer than 177,000 people were recorded as having taken shelter from the blitz in the tubes on September 17, 1940. This number fell, stabilising for a time at about 60,000 per night, then increased again when the blitz came back in 1943-44. Often troops, who were moving across London at night time, sheltered in these tube stations too.

In all, 79 deep tube platforms were permitted for use as shelters. As the years went by, proper sanitary arrangements, better lighting and facilities were arranged by the Government.

Food was provided and sold by J. Lyons of Cadby Hall and its serving was organised by the Tube Refreshment Service, which employed between 400 and 500 women. The food was delivered to the packing depots at the end of each line. At 1 p.m. each day the Tube Refreshment trains were loaded and, as the trains ran through, the bins were dropped off at a service point on each platform. At 4 p.m. wash boilers were switched on and by 6 p.m. tea and cocoa were served to the shelterers along the platform. Wherever possible, hot drinks were served again in the morning before people left for work or home.

Even on VE-night 12,000 people were at the Underground Tube stations and in the deep shelters.

The recipes that follow give a idea of the food that was sold to the shelterers and which they would have enjoyed on VE-night..

COLD MEAT PASTIES

PREPARATION TIME: 25 MINUTES

COOKING TIME: 20 MINUTES

QUANTITY: 4 PASTIES

This recipe comes from a wartime book published by McDougalls. The high amount of Worcestershire sauce, which may be reduced, if liked, is typical of recipes of the era, as people tried to put as much flavour as possible into fairly flavourless food.

Shortcrust pastry made with 8 oz (225 g) flour etc. (page 42)

For the filling:

8 oz (225 g) cold meat, minced

1 small onion, minced or chopped

2 tomatoes, sliced

2 tablespoons chopped cooked carrots or other vegetables

2 tablespoons Worcestershire sauce

2 tablespoons gravy or water

salt and pepper

1 reconstituted dried egg or fresh egg, if available, to glaze

Preheat the oven to 200°C (400°F), Gas Mark 6. Grease a baking tray.

Roll out the pastry and cut it into four rounds. Brush the edges with water or a little beaten egg. Mix the ingredients for the filling together and put in the centre of each round. Bring the edges together, pinch well and trim into flutes between the finger and thumb.

Make a slit in the side of the pastry with a pointed knife. Brush with beaten egg, if liked. Place on the baking tray and bake in the preheated oven for 20 minutes.

VEGETABLE PASTIES

Follow the recipe for Cold Meat Pasties above, but fill the pastry with about 1 lb (450 g) lightly cooked diced vegetables, such as onions, carrots, turnips, potatoes

and swede. 1-2 chopped uncooked tomatoes give extra flavour. Use less Worcestershire sauce and a little tomato ketchup to flavour.

SAVOURY POTATO PASTIES

Follow the recipe for Cold Meat Pasties but make a filling with 12 oz (350 g) diced cooked potatoes, 2 finely chopped cooked onions, 1-2 oz (25-50 g) grated cheese, 1 teaspoon finely chopped sage or ½ teaspoon dried sage and 2-3 finely chopped fresh or well-drained bottled tomatoes.

APPLE TURNOVERS

PREPARATION TIME: 25 MINUTES

COOKING TIME: 25-30 MINUTES

QUANTITY: 4 TURNOVERS

Shortcrust pastry made with 10 oz (300 g) flour etc. (page 42)
2 teaspoons semolina
For the filling:
1 lb (450 g) apples, peeled, cored and thinly sliced
1-2 oz (25-50 g) sugar
1-2 oz (25-50 g) sultanas, if available
pinch ground ginger(optional)

Preheat the oven to 200°C (400°F), Gas Mark 6. Grease a baking tray.

Roll out the pastry and cut it into four rounds. Brush the edges with water. Sprinkle the semolina over the centre of the pastry; this absorbs the juice from the apples and helps to keep the pastry crisp.

Blend the ingredients for the filling together. Put on one side only of each round. Damp the edges of the pastry with water and fold the pastry over the apple filling. Seal the edges firmly together and flute them with a finger and thumb.

Place on the baking tray and bake in the preheated oven for 20 minutes, then lower the heat to 180°C (350°F), Gas Mark 4 and cook for a further 10 minutes to make sure the fruit is tender.

Variation: If using bottled apple slices, drain them very well before using. The fruit needs a little less cooking so allow 20-25 minutes only in the oven.

CURRANT BUNS

PREPARATION TIME: 30 MINUTES, PLUS PROVING

COOKING TIME: 12-15 MINUTES

QUANTITY: 12-15 BUNS

Yeast cookery was much more popular among country-dwellers than those living in towns, although gradually they began to appreciate the fact that yeast buns were wonderfully low in fat content. The dried yeast described in the method below was the type that was available in 1945.

½ oz (15 g) fresh yeast or ¼ oz (7 g or ½ tablespoon) dried yeast
1-2 oz (25-50 g) sugar
7½ fl oz (225 ml) water
12 oz (350 g) plain flour
pinch salt
1-2 oz (25-50 g) margarine or cooking fat
2 oz (50 g) currants
To glaze:
2 tablespoons water
2 tablespoons sugar

For fresh yeast, cream the yeast with a teaspoon sugar. Warm the liquid until tepid, then add to the yeast.

If using dried yeast, dissolve 1 teaspoon of the sugar in the tepid liquid, add the dried yeast, leave for 10 minutes then use as fresh yeast.

Add a sprinkling of the flour to the yeast liquid, then leave it in a warm place until the surface is covered with bubbles.

Meanwhile, sift the flour and salt into a mixing bowl, rub in the margarine or cooking fat, add the rest of the

sugar and the currants then the yeast liquid. Mix the ingredients together then turn on to a floured board. Knead the dough well. To tell if it is sufficiently kneaded press with a floured finger: the impression comes out when the dough is ready to prove (rise).

Return the dough to a clean bowl, cover and leave in a warm place for about 1½ hours, or until just double in size.

Turn out, knead again and cut into 12-15 portions. Form into rounds. Put on to lightly greased baking trays. Cover lightly and leave to prove again for about 20 minutes or until well-risen. Preheat the oven to 220°C (425°F), Gas Mark 7. Bake the buns in the preheated oven for 12-15 minutes or until golden brown and firm.

Heat the water and blend with the sugar; brush over the buns when cooked to glaze them.

Variation: Swiss Buns: form the dough into about 15-18 finger shapes. Bake as above, but do not glaze the buns. When they are cold, cover the tops with Glacé icing (page 47).

If using modern dried yeast, add it to the flour. The strict routine for wartime dried yeast is unnecessary.

THE FORCES VICTORY

› one who can remember the day the Second World War was declared in ›tember 1939 will forget how one by one the leaders of the Commonwealth ›ntries pledged their support. They were our Allies in the fight.

Although the USA did not enter the war until after the Japanese attack on Pearl ›rbour in December 1941, individual Americans came over to form the Eagle ›uadron of the RAF. Often, too, you would see people wearing the standard uni- ›m of the British forces, then notice a flash on their arm which showed they were ›lish, Czech, Norwegian, French or some other nationality.

The celebrations in every country when the war was ended were wholehearted. ›he country had been occupied by the enemy the people had to celebrate in spirit, ›ther than with a lavish meal, for they were desperately short of food. To pay trib- ›e to all the Allied forces, this chapter gives famous dishes from some of the coun- ›es from where these brave men and women came. Sadly, lack of space prevents ›e inclusion of each and every country.

GUILDHALL CELEBRATIONS

The archives of the Guildhall show that special celebrations were given by the Corporation of London for prominent war-time officers of His Majesty's and Allied forces when they were presented with the Freedom of the City. Although details of the occasions have been carefully recorded, and dinners were held at the Guildhall, there are no details of the menus. In view of the food shortages at the time it is fairly certain that the meals would have been somewhat spartan. Famous names in the Guildhall records include General Eisenhower, who was honoured with an address and a sword of honour on 12 June 1945; General Montgomery (known often as Monty and created Viscount Montgomery of Alamein), who was given the Freedom of the City in July 1946; and Lord Louis Mountbatten (later Earl Mountbatten of Burma), on 10 July 1946.

A luncheon was given at the Guildhall for the officers and ratings of HMAS *Australia* on 17 July 1945 and, a year later, in August 1946, for officers and men of the French Navy.

AFRICA

There are four recipes typical of Africa. For South Africa I have chosen one of their interesting traditional stews made with mutton or lamb, known as Bredie. This is very good with sweet potatoes, a favourite vegetable in Africa. My husband served for a short time towards the end of the war in West Africa at Accra, Kano, and Maidugari, so I am including a recipe for the dish he enjoyed in celebration of VE Day in West Africa. There is also a recipe from Rhodesia (now Zimbabwe), and one from Kenya.

BREDIE

PREPARATION TIME: 30 MINUTES

COOKING TIME: 1¼ OR 2 HOURS (SEE METHOD)

QUANTITY: 4-6 HELPINGS

This is a traditional South African stew made with mutton or lamb. The traditional flavouring for this stew comes from a flower known as waterblommetjie, which is only available in South Africa. Rosemary makes a good substitute, however. As mutton is rarely available in Britain these days, I have given lamb in the ingredients. If mutton is used, the stew will need to be cooked for rather longer.

2 breasts of lamb, weighing about 3 lb (1.3 kg) or 8 lamb chops
pinch ground ginger, optional
salt and pepper
1-2 teaspoons brown sugar (see method)
1 oz (25 g) flour
1-2 tablespoons oil (see method)
2 medium onions, thinly sliced
1 medium cooking apple, peeled, cored and sliced
1 lb (450 g) tomatoes, skinned and chopped
½ pint (300 ml) lamb stock
1-2 teaspoons chopped rosemary ,or ½ teaspoon dried rosemary

Cut the breast of lamb into small pieces, or ask the butcher to do this for you. Blend the ginger, if used, with the seasoning, sugar and flour. (Use the larger amount of sugar with the fatter breast of lamb.) Coat the lamb with the mixture.

Heat the oil in a large frying pan. (Use the smaller amount of oil with breast of lamb, or, if there is a fair amount of fat, on the lamb chops.) Fry the meat in the hot oil until golden on both sides, then remove from the pan on to a plate. Add the onions and apple and turn in any oil remaining in the pan until they are slightly golden in colour.

Return the meat to the pan with the tomatoes, stock and rosemary, stir well, then put the lid on the saucepan. If this is a poor fit place a piece of foil underneath, as it is important that the small amount of liquid does not boil away. Simmer for 2 hours for breast of lamb, or 1½ hours for lamb chops.

Chicken Chop

Preparation time: 35 minutes

Cooking time: 2 hours

Quantity: 4-6 helpings

When VE Day was declared my husband was the Commanding Officer of three staging posts for the RAF in West Africa and he celebrated this splendid occasion with one of his favourite meals from this part of the world - a good curry.

1 chicken, weighing 4 lb (1.8 kg)
1 small lemon
2 tablespoons groundnut or sunflower oil
2 small onions, chopped
To flavour the curry:
1 large red chilli pepper or
½ teaspoon chilli powder
¼ teaspoon cayenne pepper
½ teaspoon turmeric
2 tablespoons grated fresh ginger
½ pint (300 ml) stock
½ pint (300 ml) coconut milk (see note)
1 x 2 inch (5 cm) piece cinnamon stick
salt and pepper
4 oz (100 g) fresh dates (weight when stoned)

Cut the chicken into small joints; grate the lemon zest and squeeze out the juice. Heat the oil and fry the chicken with the onions until pale golden. Remove from the pan. Chop the red chilli pepper and mix it (or the chilli powder) with the cayenne, turmeric and ginger. Add to the pan, then blend in the chicken stock. Return the chicken and onions to the pan with the lemon rind and half the lemon juice.

Put the coconut milk, cinnamon stick, seasoning and dates into the pan. Stir well to blend. Cover the pan tightly, lower the heat and simmer for 2 hours. Remove the cinnamon and add more lemon juice if required. Serve with rice, a sweet chutney and a few extra dates.

Note: to make coconut milk at home, either: (1) add 3 oz (75 g) creamed coconut to ½ pint (300 ml) boiling water and stir until dissolved; or (2) put 2 oz (50 g) desiccated coconut in a container, add ½ pint (300 ml) boiling water. Allow to stand until cold then strain and use the liquid.

Stuffed Aubergines

Preparation time: 25 minutes

Cooking time: 40 minutes

Quantity: 4 helpings

In Kenya, as in many parts of Africa, aubergines (often called garden eggs) are very plentiful.

Wash 2 large aubergines and cut in half lengthways. Scoop out the pulp and dice this. Fry a finely chopped onion in a little fat, add the aubergine pulp, 2 skinned and chopped tomatoes, 8 oz (225 g) minced lamb, 2 oz (50 g) breadcrumbs and seasoning. Put into the aubergine shells. Top with crisp breadcrumbs and a little melted butter.

Bake for 30 minutes in a preheated oven, set to 190°C (375°F) Gas Mark 5.

Banana Pudding

Preparation time: 15 minutes

Cooking time: 15-20 minutes

Quantity: 4 helpings

This simple-to-make fruit pudding is a favourite in Zimbabwe (formerly Southern Rhodesia).

Peel 4 large bananas and put them into a buttered dish. Top with the juice of 1 large orange and 2 tablespoons of brown sugar.

Cover with 2 oz (50 g) freshly grated coconut and bake in a preheated oven, set to 190°C (375°F), Gas Mark 5 for 15-20 minutes.

Variation: Desiccated coconut could be used instead of the freshly grated nut.

AUSTRALIA AND NEW ZEALAND

Undoubtedly one of the foods that returning members of the Australian and New Zealand Forces would have been given was a really good steak or even the Carpet Bag version. New Zealanders would doubtless appreciate these, too, or would have chosen a succulent leg of roast lamb or hogget (year-old lamb).

A Pavlova would have been the inevitable dessert in both countries. This delicious light sweet, based on egg whites and named after the ballerina Anna Pavlova, is one of their most prized dishes.

If friends were dropping in for a cup of tea or morning coffee to meet the returning men or women, they would no doubt have been given the very light authentic scones known as Gems and the chocolate-coated Lamingtons - both favourite recipes of Australia and New Zealand.

Gems

PREPARATION TIME: 15 MINUTES

COOKING TIME: 10 MINUTES

QUANTITY: MAKES 12

These small sweet scones are famous in Australia where they were baked in special gem irons, much cherished by their owners. Deep patty tins can be used instead. Gems freeze well.

4 oz (110 g*) self-raising flour or plain flour sifted with 1 teaspoon baking powder
pinch salt
1½ oz (40 g) butter
1½ oz (40 g) caster sugar
1 egg - size 2 or 3
4 fl oz (120 ml*) milk
***use this metrication**

Preheat the oven to 200°C (400°F), Gas Mark 6. Grease 12 gem irons or deep patty tins. Place in the oven to become very hot. Sift the flour, or flour and baking powder, and salt. Cream the butter and sugar until soft and light, beat the egg with the milk. Fold into the creamed mixture together with the flour.

Spoon into the hot irons or tins and bake for 10 minutes, or until well risen and firm. Remove on to a wire cooling rack.

"Cawfee?"

Pavlova

PREPARATION TIME: 25 MINUTES
COOKING TIME: 50 MINUTES OR SEE NOTE
QUANTITY: 6 HELPINGS

4 egg whites
8 oz (225 g) caster sugar
1½ level teaspoons cornflour
1½ teaspoons white vinegar
1 teaspoon vanilla essence

Brush one or more baking trays with a few drops of oil, or use non-stick trays or line trays with baking parchment. Make a circle of the required size on the baking parchment. The secret of a Pavlova with the crisp outside but soft, rather like a light-textured marshmallow inside, is to put the meringue shape into an oven preheated to a higher temperature then immediately alter this to the lower setting. As the heat drops in a gas oven quickly, a higher setting can be used than in an electric oven. Preheat an electric oven to 180°C (350°F), then lower to 150°C (300°F); preheat a gas oven to Mark 7 then lower to Mark 2.

Put the egg whites into a large bowl. Whisk by hand or with an electric mixer until stiff; you should be able to turn the bowl upside down without the mixture falling out. Do not whisk until the egg whites are dry and crumbly. Blend the sugar and cornflour; beat into the egg whites a tablespoon at a time. Fold the vinegar and essence into the meringue. Spoon or pipe into a flan shape. Place in the preheated oven, as described above. Lower the heat and bake for approximately 50 minutes, or until crisp on the outside and a pale beige colour. Cool in the oven with the heat turned off, then fill (see suggestions below).

The Pavlova does not store well.

Australian Filling: blend the pulp of passion fruit with whipped cream and use in the Pavlova, top with a little more passion fruit pulp.

New Zealand Filling: blend whipped cream with peeled and diced kiwifruit, top with more sliced kiwifruit. In 1945 this fruit was known as Chinese Gooseberries.

Note: for a crisp texture throughout, omit the vinegar and cornflour. Make the meringue, shape the Pavlova but preheat the oven to 90-110°C (200-225°F), Gas Mark S or ¼. Slightly quicker baking sets the outside and gives a stickier centre, in which case set the oven to 110-120°C (225-250°F), Gas Mark ¼-½. Bake for 3-4 hours. This Pavlova stores well in an airtight tin.

Lamingtons

These chocolate-coated sponge cakes are a great favourite in both Australia and New Zealand.

Make the sponge mixture as the Victoria Sandwich on page 107 with 6 oz (175 g) butter or margarine etc.

Bake in an 8 inch (20 cm) square tin in a preheated oven, set to 180°C (350°F), Gas Mark 4 for 20-25 minutes. Allow to cool then cut into 16 squares.

Insert a skewer into each square and dip in chocolate icing (see below) then coat in desiccated coconut.

Chocolate Icing

Blend 8 oz (225 g) sifted icing sugar with 1 oz (25 g) cocoa powder, put into a saucepan with 2 tablespoons water, few drops vanilla essence and ½ oz (15 g) butter. Heat until a flowing consistency. Use the icing before it has time to stiffen.

THE USA AND CANADA

In many American homes there might well have been two Thanksgiving dinners in 1945. One in November, the month the event is generally celebrated, and the second, a very special celebration, in either May for VE Day or August for VJ Day.

The main dish for the real Thanksgiving is roast turkey and the most popular dessert a Pumpkin Pie. As both the Victory Days took place in spring to summertime, when soft fruit was available, I have included a recipe for the American well-loved Strawberry Shortcake instead of the pie.

Roast turkey is so well known, I have included another American favourite dish of the era - Chicken Maryland. This became extremely popular in Britain during the late 1950s and early 1960s.

Canadians love dishes with maple syrup and Maple Pancakes would be a wonderful welcome home dish.

Chicken Maryland

This combination of fried chicken, sweetcorn fritters and fried bananas was a great favourite.

Coat 4 tender chicken joints with seasoned flour then beaten egg and crisp breadcrumbs. Fry for approximately 15 minutes in hot fat or oil until golden brown and cooked.

Keep hot while frying the sweetcorn fritters (see below) and bananas.

Peel 4 bananas, coat in seasoned flour and fry for a few minutes.

Sweetcorn Fritters

Blend 2 oz (50 g) self-raising flour with a little seasoning, 1 egg and 3 tablespoons milk. Add 6 oz (175 g) drained canned or cooked sweetcorn kernels.

Fry in hot fat or oil until brown and firm. Drain on absorbent paper.

Maple Pancakes

Canadians, like Americans, enjoy these at most times of the day.

Make a batter with 4 oz (110 g*) flour, pinch salt, 2 eggs and 14 fl oz (500 ml) milk. Cook in the usual way and top with a generous helping of maple syrup.

A slightly thicker batter can be used to make waffles.

*use this metrication.

Strawberry Shortcake

Preparation time: 20 minutes

Cooking time: 10 or 15-20 minutes

Quantity: 4-6 helpings

There are many recipes for shortcakes, this one is not only a popular one in America, but it would have been the most usual in 1945, for the people in that country were rationed for fats, and this particular recipe uses relatively little.

For the shortcake mixture:

3 oz (85 g*) butter or margarine

8 oz (225 g) self-raising flour or plain flour sifted with 2 teaspoons baking powder

4 oz (100 g) caster sugar

1 egg - size 1 or 2

milk, to bind

For the filling:

1 lb (450 g) strawberries

sugar to taste

little butter

***use this metrication**

Preheat the oven to 220°C (425°F), Gas Mark 7. Lightly grease a large baking tray. Sift the flour, or flour and baking powder. Rub the butter or margarine into the flour, add the sugar. Beat the egg, add to the flour mixture with sufficient milk to make a soft rolling consistency. Roll, or pat out, the dough until ¼ inch (0.5 cm) thick and cut into 8-12 rounds for smaller individual shortcakes. If making one large shortcake, divide the dough into equal halves and form each into an 8 inch (20 cm) round. Place on the baking tray and put in the preheated oven. Bake small shortcakes for about 10 minutes and large ones for 15-20 minutes, or until they are well risen, firm and brown.

Slice most of the strawberries and add sugar to taste. Save a few whole berries for decoration. When the shortcakes are cool, sandwich together with a little butter and the sliced strawberries. Top with the whole fruit. Serve the shortcakes when freshly made, with cream or yogurt or fromage frais.

Variation: Omit the butter when sandwiching the shortcakes together, use sliced strawberries only, top with whipped cream and serve with the coulis below.

Strawberry Coulis

Heat 2 oz (50 g) caster sugar with 1 tablespoon lemon juice and 1 tablespoon water until dissolved. Sieve or liquidize 1 lb (450 g) of strawberries. Blend with the syrup. Serve cold or heat for a short time. Do not overcook or you will lose the fresh fruit flavour.

FAR EAST

VJ Day in August 1945 brought the fighting in the Far East to an end. This had involved a vast number of the Allied forces fighting the Japanese. Many people, including both those in the armed forces and civilians, had been taken prisoner. It is not hard to imagine their relief when the fighting ended with the capitulation of Japan.

Oriental dishes were little known in Britain at that time but they have, of course, become great favourites since. On the following pages are three recipes from the Far East. It is doubtful if Service personnel sampled them at the time, since they had relatively little to eat, especially those who had been prisoners of war.

Sin Tim Yue

This Chinese dish is very easily prepared. Use a firm-fleshed fish.

Cut 1½ lb (675 g) white fish into 1.5 inch (3.5 cm) pieces. Dry well and coat in a good tablespoon cornflour seasoned with salt and pepper.

Cut 4 oz (100 g) green beans and about 8 spring onions into small pieces; peel and crush 2 garlic cloves.

Deseed a red pepper; drain 2 oz (50 g) canned bamboo shoots and 2 oz (50 g) water chestnuts; cut these, and the pepper, into matchstick pieces.

Heat 1½ tablespoons vegetable oil in a wok or large frying pan and cook the fish until golden in colour. Lift on to a hot dish and keep hot.

Add another 1½ tablespoons oil to the pan and fry the prepared vegetables for 3-4 minutes.

Blend 1½ teaspoons cornflour with 2 tablespoons soy sauce, 2 tablespoons white wine, 1 tablespoon lemon juice, 1 tablespoon caster sugar and 1 or 2 teaspoons chopped fresh ginger.

Pour over the vegetables, stir over a low heat until thickened. Spoon over the hot fish and serve with cooked bean sprouts.

Marta Pulao

On VE Day in May 1945 my brother, an officer in the Merchant Navy, was on a ship bound for India with military equipment. On VJ Day he was in Bombay with the ship loaded ready for a Malaysian invasion which fortunately did not happen, due to Japan's capitulation. The ship's crew had changed to Indians and this may well be one of the dishes they would have eaten on the important day.

Soak 6-7 oz (175-200 g) Patna rice in cold water for 1 hour. Heat 1½ oz (40 g) ghee (clarified butter) and add 6 cloves, 2 small pieces of cinnamon, ½ teaspoon turmeric and a teaspoon caraway seeds. Fry in the ghee for 2 minutes to bring out the flavours. Drain the rice, add to the pan with a little salt and 8 oz (225 g) shelled peas.

Mix well and cook gently for 4-5 minutes then add 2 pints (1.2 litres) boiling water. Allow the rice mixture to reach boiling point then cover the pan tightly and cook for about 30 minutes. This goes well with all meat and vegetable dishes.

Shrimps in Lime and Coconut Sauce

PREPARATION TIME: 15 MINUTES PLUS MARINATING

COOKING TIME: 6 MINUTES

QUANTITY: 4 HELPINGS

This recipe, which is typical of East Asian dishes, is included in tribute to the many people who suffered great deprivation at Singapore and in that region.

1 large or 2 small limes
1 lb (450 g) peeled prawns or shrimps
½ pint (300 ml) coconut milk (see below)
1 tablespoon sunflower oil
2 teaspoons light soy sauce
salt and pepper
little chopped lemon grass or parsley, to garnish

Grate the top zest from the limes and squeeze out enough juice to give 2 tablespoons, or a little more if preferred. Blend the fish with the lime zest. Cover and leave in the refrigerator for an hour so the lime flavour penetrates the shellfish.

Make the coconut milk: the simplest and best way for this recipe is to pour ½ pint (300 ml) boiling water over 2 oz (50 g) desiccated coconut. Leave until cold then put into a liquidizer to make a smooth liquid. You can also heat 3 oz (75 g) creamed coconut in ½ pint (300 ml) water until dissolved and use this.

Heat the oil, toss the shellfish in it for 1 or 2 minutes, then add the coconut milk, soy sauce and lime juice. Season to taste and heat thoroughly, but do not allow the mixture to boil.

Top with the lemon grass or parsley and serve with cooked rice.

OCCUPIED EUROPE

The following recipes represent the countries, many of whose people served with Allied forces or were resistance fighters, in various parts of Europe. In Russia returning troops would be facing devastation in many of their towns and villages but would know that their country was once again free of occupying troops after VE Day. Solyanka is one of their most delicious soups and a Borshch is both economical and full of flavour.

Czechoslovakia, Poland, Hungary and Norway had known the horrors of German occupation. Sadly, none of these countries was to enjoy complete freedom immediately after VE Day in 1945; they had to wait for a long time for this to come. The underground movement in the occupied countries and the bravery of their people who fought alongside the Allies was greatly admired.

The recipes from these countries which I have included here are all very easy to make and give several new ways with vegetables.

My sister married a Norwegian and has sent me the information about this country at the time of VE Day.

Solyanka

PREPARATION TIME: 25 MINUTES

COOKING TIME: 20-25 MINUTES

QUANTITY: 6 HELPINGS

This is a wonderful fish soup that is sufficiently sustaining to make a complete meal. Although the ideal choice of fish is given in the ingredients, the fish can be varied according to what is available.

2 tablespoons oil
1 onion, finely chopped
2 small carrots, neatly diced
2 small potatoes, neatly diced
2 pints (1.2 litres) fish stock
salt and pepper
1 bay leaf
1 lb (450 g) lightly cooked salmon
8 oz (225 g) lightly cooked white fish
2 large pickled cucumbers, thinly sliced
1 tablespoon capers
1 lemon
To garnish:
¼ pint (150 ml) soured cream or yogurt
1 tablespoon chopped parsley
dill sprigs
green olives, stoned
6 lemon slices

Heat the oil in a saucepan, add the onion, carrots and potatoes and cook for 5 minutes, stirring from time to time. Add the fish stock, season lightly, then add the bay leaf and simmer for 10 minutes.

Cut the fish into 1-1½ inch (2.5-3.5 cm) pieces, add to the soup with the cucumbers and capers. Heat gently for 5-10 minutes. Halve the lemon, discard the pips, then scoop out the pulp and add to the soup.

Pour into soup bowls, top with the soured cream or yogurt, parsley, dill, olives and lemon slices.

Borshch

This can be made quickly with cooked beetroot but the flavour is much better if an uncooked one is chosen. This recipe gives 4-6 helpings.

Peel and grate a large raw beetroot, grate about 8 oz (225 g) carrots. Peel and slice an onion and garlic clove, skin and chop 2 large tomatoes; chop 1 celery stick.

Put all the vegetables into 2 pints (1.2 litres) of beef stock, add 1-2 tablespoons vinegar and 1-2 tablespoons lemon juice with salt and pepper to taste. Simmer for about 1½ hours.

Top each serving with soured cream.

Variation: If using cooked beetroot simmer the other vegetables for about 35 minutes, add the peeled and grated cooked beetroot and cook for 10 minutes then serve topped with the soured cream.

Pacuszki z Kartofli

These Polish Potato Pancakes are delicious. This recipe will make 4-6 servings.

Boil about 1½ lb (675 g) potatoes, strain, sieve and mash until very smooth.

Separate 3 eggs and gradually beat into the potato mixture the 3 egg yolks, ½ pint (300 ml) milk, a little ground cinnamon and sugar to taste.

Whisk the 3 egg whites until stiff and fold them into the mixture.

Heat butter in a frying pan and fry spoonfuls of the mixture for 2 or 3 minutes then turn over and cook on the other side for the same time.

Serve as soon as possible after cooking, topped with cooked berry fruits or with hot jam.

Letscho

PREPARATION TIME: 20 MINUTES

COOKING TIME: 50 MINUTES

QUANTITY: 4 HELPINGS

This Hungarian dish is a pleasant change from the more familiar French Ratatouille.

2 medium onions, thinly sliced
2 oz (50 g) lard or cooking fat
2-3 green peppers, deseeded and sliced
4 large tomatoes, skinned and sliced
salt and pepper

Separate the onion slices into rings. Heat the lard or fat and cook the onions until tender but not brown. Add the sliced peppers and tomatoes with a little seasoning. Cover the pan and cook gently for 35-50 minutes.

Serve as a separate course or with meat or fish.

Kulajda

PREPARATION TIME: 20 MINUTES

COOKING TIME: 30 MINUTES

QUANTITY: 4 HELPINGS

This Czechoslovakian dish is an original potato soup, for when it is almost ready to serve an egg is added for each person. These are heated sufficiently to set lightly, so you eat a whole egg with your soup.

1 lb (450 g) potatoes, weight when peeled and diced
1¼ pints (750 ml) water
salt and pepper
1-2 teaspoons caraway seeds
1 medium onion, finely chopped
3-4 oz (75-100 g) mushrooms, finely diced
1 tablespoon flour
½ pint (300 ml) single cream
4 eggs
1 teaspoon lemon juice or vinegar

Put the potatoes into a rather wide saucepan with the water, seasoning, caraway seeds and onion. Simmer for 10 minutes, then add the mushrooms. Cover the pan and simmer for a further 15 minutes, or until the potatoes are soft. Blend the flour with the cream, whisk into the hot, but not boiling soup, heat very gently until the soup is hot again.

Carefully break the eggs into the soup and cook for a few minutes until they are lightly set. Finally stir in the lemon juice or vinegar.

Spoon an egg and some soup into individual soup cups or soup bowls.

NORWAY

The picture on this page shows the jubilation felt throughout Norway on VE Day 1945. Nothing could stop the happiness of Oslo's inhabitants - not even an armed German soldier.

This scene was typical of all the freed countries of occupied Europe in 1945.

In Norway by 1945 the inhabitants were on the verge of starvation, for the Germans sent the best food back to Germany. There was no tea or coffee, and all kinds of weird substitutes such as the dried leaves of various bushes or dried apple peel were used. Leather was very scarce and many people wore shoes which they had made out of paper or fish skins.

Even people living in flats tried to keep a few rabbits or chickens to eke out the meagre food supplies.

Blotkake

Preparation time: 15 minutes

Cooking time: 30 minutes

Makes: 1 cake

This light cake, smothered with whipped cream and berry fruit, often lingonberries or cloudberries, is a popular feature of Norwegian celebrations, so would have been made in Norway just as soon as all the ingredients were available.

4 eggs
8 oz (225 g) caster sugar
2 oz (50 g) plain flour
2 oz (50 g) potato flour, or more plain flour
1 teaspoon baking powder
For filling and topping:
½-¾ pint (300-450 ml) whipping cream
berry fruits

Preheat the oven to 180°C(350°F), Gas Mark 4. Grease and flour or line a 9 inch (23 cm) round cake tin.

Whisk the eggs and sugar until thick and creamy. Sift the flour(s) with the baking powder, and fold into the egg mixture. Spoon into the tin and bake for 30 minutes or until firm to a gentle touch.

Cool for a time, then turn out. When cold, cut into 3 layers. Whip the cream. Fill and top the cake with the cream and berries.

COUNTRY CELEBRATIONS

Throughout Britain farmers had worked ceaselessly to cultivate crops, rear livestock and produce the best yields of milk to feed Britain. Their contribution to our war effort was of great importance for it was essential that we relied as much as possible on our own resources of food.

From the point of view of feeding their families, country people were perhaps a little more fortunate than town-dwellers, for they could catch rabbits, pigeons and game birds when in season. On the other hand, they may not have been able to buy the extra buns and cakes from bakers as easily, if they lived a long way from the shop, or visit British restaurants or other restaurants, for their work gave them little leisure. The cooks of the family had to depend upon their own cooking and baking skills.

Although the years ahead of 1945 would still be busy ones for the farming communities, they, like the rest of Britain, celebrated VE and VJ Days in 1945 with their families and friends.

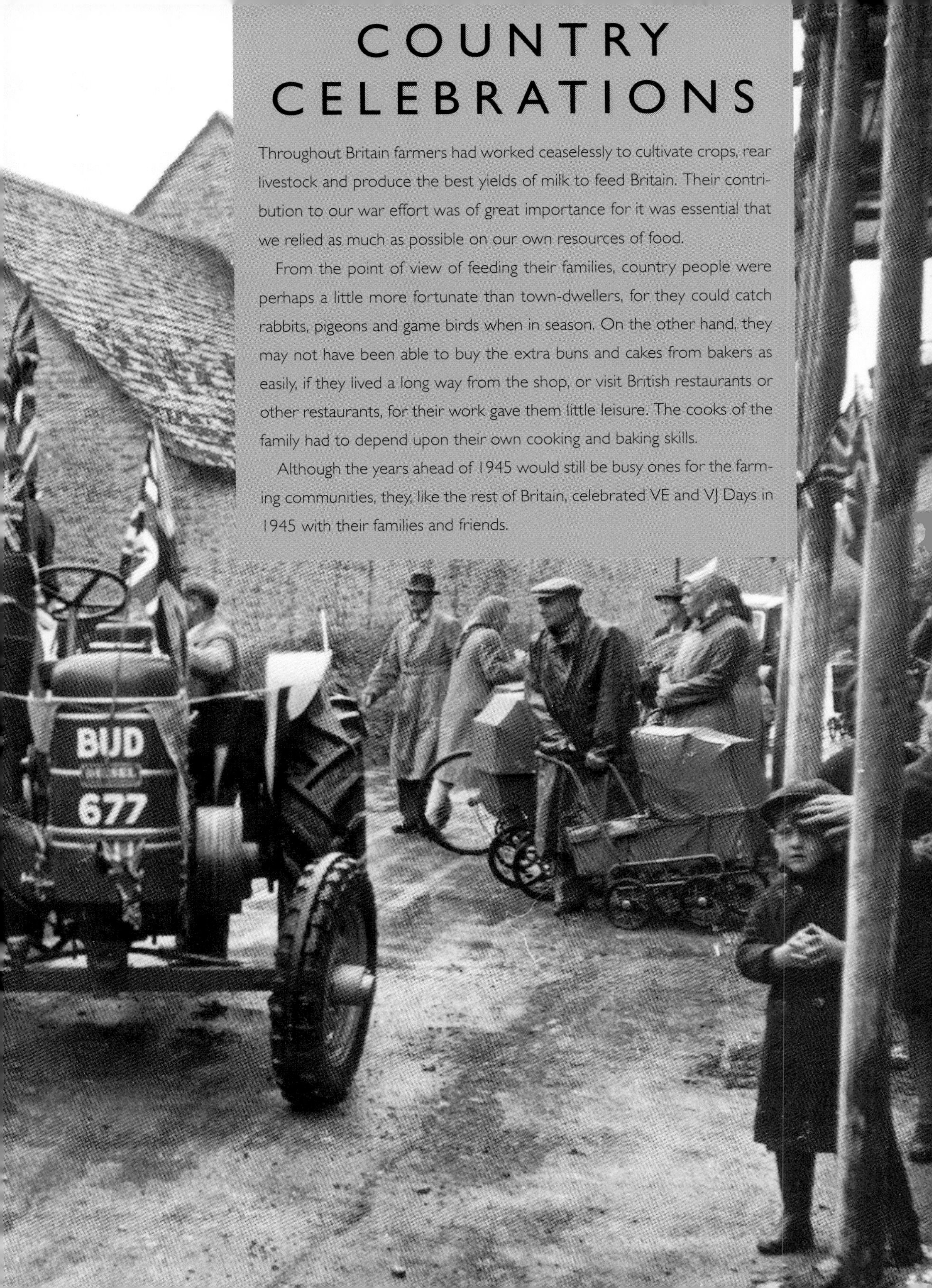

For a healthy, happy job
Join the
WOMEN'S
LAND
ARMY
CLIVE UPTTON
For details:
APPLY TO NEAREST W.L.A. COUNTY OFFICE OR TO W.L.A. HEADQUARTERS 6 CHESHAM ~~PLACE~~ LONDON S.W.1
STREET
Issued by the Ministry of Agriculture and the Ministry of Labour and National Service
PRINTED FOR H.M. STATIONERY OFFICE BY W. R. ROYLE & SON LTD

THE WOMEN'S LAND ARMY

One of the hardest-working groups of women in the country was the Women's Land Army. They replaced the younger male farm and agricultural workers, who were serving in the Forces or in factories on essential work. The women's days were long and full of hard physical effort; it was amazing how young girls, who had little, if any, experience of the hard work of farming in all weathers, managed so well. Victory meant they could return to their homes, though many continued to work on the land after the war was over.

Much less well-known than the Women's Land Army, the Women's Timber Corps (WTC), known as the Lumberjills, numbered more than 6,000 members at its peak. They tackled every sort of job connected with wood and trees; they drove tractors and locomotives, hauling loads of timber up and down impossible gradients. They measured and felled trees and loaded endless telegraph poles, pitprops, railway sleepers and potential packing cases and charcoal.

KIDNEY AND BACON SOUP

PREPARATION TIME: 25 MINUTES

COOKING TIME: 55 MINUTES

QUANTITY: 4-6 HELPINGS

This is a very satisfying soup, nutritious enough to make a light meal. As most farmers kept pigs they would be able to use the kidneys plus their allowance of bacon in it.

2 pig's kidneys, skinned and finely diced
1 oz (25 g) flour
salt and pepper
3 bacon rashers, derinded and chopped
2 medium leeks, thinly sliced
4 oz (100 g) mushrooms, sliced
1½ pints (900 ml) water
3 slices of bread
2 tablespoons chopped chives

Remove any gristle from the kidneys. Blend the flour and seasoning and coat the kidneys in this. Heat the bacon and bacon rinds in a saucepan, add the kidneys and cook gently for 5 minutes, then add the leeks and mushrooms, with the water. Stir well to blend, then lower the heat and simmer for 45 minutes, or until the kidneys are tender. Remove the bacon rinds.

Toast the bread and cut it into ½ inch (1.5 cm) dice. Serve the soup with a topping of the toasted croûtons and chopped fresh chives.

PARSLEY PUDDING

PREPARATION TIME: 25 MINUTES

COOKING TIME: 2 HOURS

QUANTITY: 4 HELPINGS

Parsley gives a very special flavour to this savoury pudding. Never waste the stalks of parsley, they can be used in soups and stews, for they give even more flavour than the leaves.

For the pudding:
8 oz (225 g) self-raising flour or plain flour sifted with 2 teaspoons baking powder
½ teaspoon salt
2 oz (50 g) raw potato, grated
2 oz (50 g) suet, finely chopped or grated
water, to bind
For the filling:
2 bacon rashers, derinded and chopped
sprinkling of gravy powder
8 tablespoons finely chopped parsley leaves

Grease a 1½ pint (900 ml) pudding basin. Sift the flour, or flour and baking powder, with the salt, add the potato and suet then enough water to make a dough with a soft rolling consistency.

Roll out the pastry and use nearly three-quarters to line the base and sides of the basin.

Add the filling ingredients, then roll out the remain-

ing pastry to form a lid; moisten the edges of the pastry with water, put the pastry round in place and seal the joins. Cover with margarine paper and/or a cloth and steam for 2 hours. Allow the water under the steamer to boil briskly for the first hour, then lower the heat for the remaining period.

Variations: for Steak and Parsley Pudding: use 8 oz (225 g) finely diced stewing steak instead of the bacon.

Bacon, Onion and Parsley Pudding: follow the recipe but add 2 sliced onions to the ingredients.

RABBIT STEW

PREPARATION TIME: 30 MINUTES

COOKING TIME: 2 HOURS

QUANTITY: 4-6 HELPINGS

1 rabbit, cut into joints
1 tablespoon vinegar
1 oz (25 g) flour
salt and pepper
1-2 oz (25-50 g) dripping or cooking fat
2 bacon rashers, derinded and chopped, if available
2 medium onions, sliced
3 medium carrots, sliced
1 pint (600 ml) water or chicken stock
¼ pint (150 ml) dry cider
½ tablespoon chopped tarragon or ½ teaspoon dried tarragon
Dumplings (page 93)
2 tablespoons chopped parsley

Put the rabbit to soak in cold water with the vinegar for 30 minutes. Remove and dry well. Mix the flour with the seasoning and coat the rabbit joints in this. Heat the dripping or cooking fat with the bacon rinds, add the rabbit and cook steadily for about 10 minutes, or until golden brown in colour. Remove from the pan, add the bacon, onions and carrots and cook for 5 minutes then return the rabbit to the pan with the water or stock, stir as the liquid comes to the boil and thickens slightly. Add the cider and the tarragon.

Cover the pan and simmer gently for about 1½ hours. Check there is sufficient liquid in the pan, if not add a little more water or stock and bring to the boil. Add the uncooked dumplings, made as in the recipe on page 93, and cook for a further 20 minutes. Remove the bacon rinds and sprinkle over the chopped parsley before serving the stew.

Variations: Chicken Stew: use a not-too-fat chicken instead of rabbit. There is no need to soak the jointed chicken. The cooking time will be about the same as the rabbit if it is a fairly elderly fowl. If the chicken is younger, then reduce the cooking time by about 15 minutes.

Pigeon Stew: use 3 large or 6 smaller pigeons. There is no need to soak these before cooking. Halve the birds then proceed as in the recipe. If the pigeons are young, reduce the cooking time by about 15-20 minutes.

RENDERING DOWN CHICKEN FAT

Allow the chicken stock to become quite cold then carefully take the fat from the top of the liquid. Put this into a saucepan, cover with cold water and bring the water to the boil. Pour into a bowl and leave in a cool place.

Lift the fat from the top of the liquid. Any impurities or tiny pieces of food will be in the liquid at the bottom of the bowl. The chicken fat can be used in cooking.

USING CHICKEN STOCK

The stock in which the chicken was cooked is excellent as a basis for soups. Store it carefully and use as soon as possible.

DUMPLINGS

PREPARATION TIME: 15 MINUTES

COOKING TIME: 15-20 MINUTES

QUANTITY: 4-6 HELPINGS

Dumplings were one of the dishes that were frequently made, for they helped to satisfy people's appetites and so 'eke out' precious meat.

Grated raw potato was used in this type of pastry as well as in shortcrust pastry to give a good texture with the minimum of fat.

8 oz (225 g) self-raising flour or plain flour sifted with 2 teaspoons baking powder
good pinch salt
2 oz (50 g) suet, finely chopped or grated
2 oz (50 g) raw potato, grated
water, to bind

Sift the flour, or flour and baking powder, with the salt, add the suet and potato. Mix well then gradually add enough cold water to make a soft rolling consistency.

Divide the mixture into about 16 and roll into balls with lightly floured hands.

Drop the dumpling balls into boiling salted water and cook briskly for 10 minutes then lower the heat and cook more slowly for a further 5-10 minutes, until the dumplings have risen well. Lift out of the water with a perforated spoon and serve.

Variations: Instead of the suet, use 1-2 oz (25-50 g) margarine or cooking fat in the dumplings. Rub this into the flour, or flour and baking powder, and salt.

Savoury Dumplings: flavour the mixture with chopped parsley, chives or sage or a little dried herbs. These are very good served by themselves and just sprinkled with grated cheese.

Mustard Dumplings: add a generous amount of mustard powder to the flour; Mustard Dumplings are particularly good with cooked chicken or rabbit.

Sweet Dumplings: add 1-2 tablespoons sugar to the mixture after adding the suet, or other fat. Boil in water, or if you have soft fruit left from cooking fruit dilute this with water and cook the dumplings in it.

If you can spare 1-2 tablespoons marmalade add this to the mixture before mixing with the water.

Top sweet dumplings with a very little sugar before serving with cooked fruit or by themselves.

Prune Sponge

PREPARATION TIME: 25 MINUTES

COOKING TIME: 1½ HOURS

QUANTITY: 4-6 HELPINGS

This is a very good pudding, for the prunes become plump with steaming. If you soak the prunes in weak left-over tea, rather than water, they will have a very rich flavour.

8-12 prunes, soaked overnight
8 oz (225 g) self-raising flour or plain flour sifted with 2 teaspoons baking powder
½ teaspoon mixed spice
½ teaspoon grated or ground nutmeg
1 oz (25 g) margarine or cooking fat
1-2 tablespoons golden syrup
6 tablespoons milk or milk and water

Grease a 1½ pint (900 ml) basin. Drain the soaked prunes and arrange at the bottom of the basin.

Sift the flour, or flour and baking powder, with the spices, rub in the margarine or cooking fat, add the golden syrup and the milk, or milk and water. Spoon into the basin, cover with margarine paper and steam for 1½ hours.

Turn the steamed pudding out and serve it with a custard sauce (see page 38).

Bread and Butter Pudding

PREPARATION TIME: 20 MINUTES

COOKING TIME: 1-1¼ HOURS

QUANTITY: 4-6 HELPINGS

The Celebrations for VE and VJ days in 1945 might well have been the time when the farmer's wife or whoever did the cooking at the farm would decide to make a real Bread and Butter Pudding with butter and shell eggs - a rare extravagance.

4 large slices of bread
approximately 2 oz (50 g) butter
3 oz (75 g) sultanas
3 eggs
2 oz (50 g) sugar
1 pint (600 ml) milk
For the topping:
sprinkling of sugar
little grated or ground nutmeg

Spread the bread with the butter and then cut into neat squares. Put into a 2 pint (1.2 litre) pie dish. Add the sultanas. Beat the eggs with the sugar. Warm the milk, pour over the beaten eggs then strain over the bread and butter. Allow to stand for at least 30 minutes.

Preheat the oven to 150°C (300°F), Gas Mark 2. Sprinkle the sugar over the top of the pudding together with the nutmeg. Bake for 1-1¼ hours or until just firm.

Variations: For a very crisp brown topping raise the oven heat to 180°C (350°F), Gas Mark 4 for the last 5-8 minutes.

Jam Bread and Butter Pudding: Spread the bread and butter with Victoria plum or apricot jam or with marmalade before cutting it into squares.

Use 3 reconstituted dried eggs instead of fresh eggs.

TURN WASTE INTO DELICACIES!

Fruit Crisp

PREPARATION TIME: 25 MINUTES

COOKING TIME: 40-45 MINUTES

QUANTITY: 4 HELPINGS

1 lb (450 g) fruit, weight when prepared, i.e. peeled or stoned
2-3 tablespoons water (see method)
1 oz (25 g) sugar
For the topping:
1 oz (25 g) margarine or cooking fat
1 oz (25 g) sugar
1 tablespoon golden syrup
4 oz (100 g) rolled oats

Preheat the oven to 180°C (350°F), Gas Mark 4. Grease a 1½ pint (900 ml) pie dish. Put the fruit into the pie dish with the water and 1 oz (25 g) sugar. If using ripe soft fruit, use only about 1 tablespoon water. Cover the pie dish and bake firm fruits for 10-15 minutes and soft fruits for 5-10 minutes.

Put the margarine or cooking fat into a saucepan, add the sugar and syrup. Stir over a low heat until the ingredients have melted. Remove from the heat and stir in the rolled oats. Blend thoroughly then spread over the fruit in a flat layer.

Bake in the preheated oven for 30 minutes, or until the topping is golden brown. Serve hot or cold.

Cheese and Apple Cake

PREPARATION TIME: 20 MINUTES

COOKING TIME: 30-35 MINUTES

QUANTITY: 1 CAKE

Farmers and their employees were allowed extra cheese since it was not possible for them to obtain canteen meals or get to British restaurants. The small amount of cheese in this cake gives it a most interesting flavour. It should be eaten when freshly baked and even slightly warm.

PLUM CHARLOTTE

Preparation time: 25 minutes, Cooking time: 40 minutes, but see method, Quantity: 4 helpings

1 lb (450 g) fruit, weight when prepared, i.e. peeled or stoned
3 oz (75 g) sugar
8 oz (225 g) bread
2 oz (50 g) margarine or suet

Cut apples into slices, halve and stone plums but leave soft fruit whole. It is advisable to cook the firm fruits for about 5 minutes in a saucepan with 1 oz (25 g) of the sugar and very little water. Soft fruit is better if not pre-cooked.

Make the bread into fairly coarse crumbs by pulling it into pieces with your fingers. If using margarine, melt it, add the crumbs and turn around in the hot margarine until coated and slightly brown. If using suet, grate it finely and mix with the crumbs. Add the remaining sugar to the bread.

Preheat the oven to 180°C (350°F), Gas Mark 4. Put half the crumb mixture into a greased 1½ pint (900 ml) pie dish and then add the fruit. Cover with the rest of the crumb mixture. Bake in the preheated oven for 35 minutes or until the crumb topping is very brown and crisp.

10 oz (300 g) self-raising flour or plain flour sifted with 2½ teaspoons baking powder
pinch salt
3 oz (75 g) margarine or cooking fat or dripping
1 oz (25 g) sugar
2 oz (50 g) Cheddar cheese, grated
¼ pint (150 ml) milk
For the topping:
4 dessert apples, peeled, cored and thinly sliced
2 oz (50 g) sugar, preferably brown
½ teaspoon ground cinnamon
1 oz (25 g) margarine, melted

Preheat the oven to 190°C (375°F), Gas Mark 5. Sift the flour, or flour and baking powder, with the salt into a mixing bowl, rub in the margarine, cooking fat or dripping, add the sugar and cheese. Mix well, then gradually blend with the milk. Turn the mixture on to a lightly floured board and knead lightly then form into an oblong to fit into an ungreased 7 x 10 inch (18 x 25 cm) Swiss Roll tin. Arrange the apple slices on top of the dough. Blend the sugar and cinnamon and sprinkle over the apples, then brush with the melted margarine.

Bake for 30-35 minutes or until firm. Cool for a few minutes then remove from the tin. Cut into fingers.

Summer Fruit Crumble

Preparation time: 20 minutes

Cooking time: 35 minutes

Quantity: 4-6 helpings

Fruit Crumbles became popular during the years of rationing when the scarcity of fat made it difficult to produce good pastry for fruit pies and tarts.

A crumble made with lovely summer fruits, such as black and red currants, raspberries or loganberries, makes a splendid special occasion pudding which is economical to make.

1½ lb (675 g) mixed summer fruits (see above)
2 oz (50 g) sugar
For the crumble topping:
6 oz (175 g) flour, plain if possible
3 oz (75 g) margarine
3-4 oz (75-100 g) sugar

Preheat the oven to 180°C (350°F), Gas Mark 4. Prepare the fruits and put into a 2 pint (1.2 litre) pie dish. Add the sugar but there is no need to add water if the fruits are ripe and juicy.

Cover the pie dish and heat the fruit in the oven for about 5 minutes only, then take out of the oven.

Put the flour into a mixing bowl, rub in the margarine, add the sugar and sprinkle evenly over the top of the fruit. Do not cover the dish. Bake for 30 minutes or until the topping is golden brown and crisp.

Variations: The amount of margarine can be reduced to 2 oz (50 g) and the sugar to 2 oz (50 g) also, but the amount of sugar in the recipe helps to give a really crisp topping.

If using firm plums or sliced apples add a little water and cook for 10-15 minutes, or until the fruit begins to soften slightly before adding the crumble topping.

If short of sugar add a little dried fruit or marmalade to help sweeten the fruit or use a sugar substitute.

Family Currant Cake

Preparation time: 20 minutes

Cooking time: 50 minutes or 1 hour

Quantity: 1 cake

8 oz (225 g) self-raising flour or plain flour sifted with 2 teaspoons baking powder
4 oz (115 g*) margarine or cooking fat
4 oz (115 g*) sugar, preferably soft light brown
1 reconstituted dried egg or fresh egg
6 oz (175 g) currants
5 tablespoons milk
*** use this metrication**

DIG FOR VICTORY

Grease and flour a 6-7 inch (15-18 cm) round cake tin or 1½-2 lb (675-900 g) loaf tin. Preheat the oven to 180°C (350°F), Gas Mark 4.

Sift the flour, or flour and baking powder, into a mixing bowl, rub in the margarine or cooking fat, add the sugar, beaten egg and the currants. Mix well, then gradually stir in the milk and mix again.

Spoon into the cake or loaf tin. Bake until firm. When baked in a loaf tin the cake will take approximately 50 minutes but about 1 hour in the round tin. Cool for a few minutes then turn out on to a wire cooling rack.

Dripping Cake

Preparation time: 15 minutes

Cooking time: 1 hour-1 hour 10 minutes

Quantity: 1 cake

Dripping was a highly prized ingredient, because it was a very flavourful form of fat which had many uses. If a family had saved their meat coupons to have a joint of beef the drippings from the roasting pan would be saved, clarified (see page 57) and allowed to become cold to use in baking.

8 oz (225 g) self-raising flour or plain flour sifted with 2 teaspoons baking powder
pinch salt
4 oz (100 g) clarified dripping (page 57)
3 oz (75 g) sugar
1 reconstituted dried or fresh egg
5 oz (150 g) dried fruit
6 tablespoons milk

Preheat the oven to 180°C (350°F), Gas Mark 4. Grease and flour a 6 inch (15 cm) cake tin. Sift the flour and salt into a mixing bowl, rub in the dripping, then add the rest of the ingredients.

Spoon into the cake tin and bake for 1 hour-1 hour 10 minutes, or until firm. Turn out on to a wire cooling rack. The richness of dripping made this economical cake keep moist for some time.

Variation: Use cooking fat instead of dripping.

Mock Almond Paste

Many cakes benefit from the addition of an icing or a topping like this almond paste. The recipe comes from a leaflet, produced by the manufacturers of Stork margarine, for an iced Victory Cake.

Sieve 4 oz (110 g - use this metrication) dried potato powder and 1 heaped tablespoon dried egg powder together.

Put 2 oz (50 g) margarine, 4½ tablespoons (about 3 oz/75 g) granulated sugar and 2 tablespoons water into a saucepan. Stir over a low heat until the margarine and sugar have melted, which should take 3 - 5 minutes. Add the potato powder and egg and stir well. Keep the heat low and continue to stir for about 3 minutes, or until thick and smooth.

Remove from the heat and stir in 1 tablespoon almond essence. (The original recipe added 1 teaspoon vanilla essence as well.) Cool, knead and roll into a round to fit the top of an 8 inch (20 cm) cake. The Almond Paste will keep for up to 4 weeks.

VICTORY OVER RATIONING

Rationing lasted for 14 years in Britain, from 1940 until 1954, far longer than any of us imagined it would. This chapter shows how the British coped with food shortages, even after the war. In fact, shortages tended to get rather worse when hostilities had ceased, for in so many parts of the world people were almost at starvation point and the world stocks of food had to go to them as well as coming to this country.

On page 100 I have listed the dates when the various rationed foods came off the ration in Britain. It may seem strange to see that bread was de-rationed in 1948, when it had not been rationed during the war. It had to be rationed in 1946, when there was a world shortage of grains.

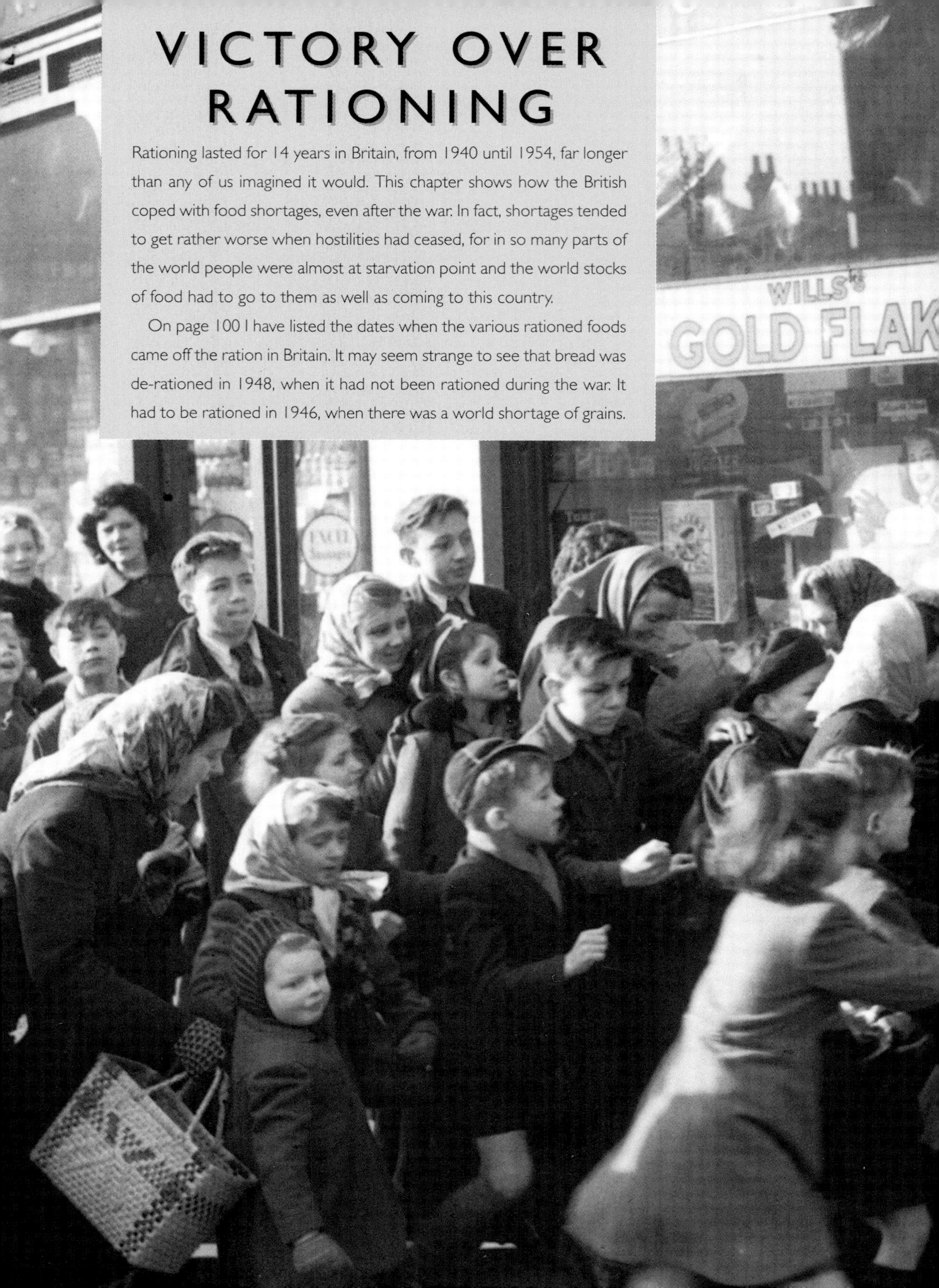

CHOCOLATE
Mrs E. Winstanley . Licensed to sell Tobacco.
AI LIGHT

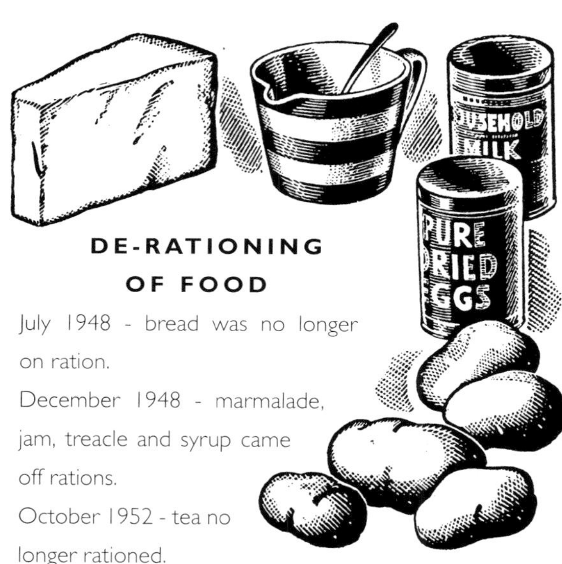

DE-RATIONING OF FOOD

July 1948 - bread was no longer on ration.

December 1948 - marmalade, jam, treacle and syrup came off rations.

October 1952 - tea no longer rationed.

February 1953 - sweets came off ration.

March 1953 - distribution of eggs no longer controlled, they were off the ration.

April 1953 - now possible to obtain cream, which had been unobtainable during the years of rationing.

September 1953 - sugar came off the ration.

May 1954 - butter, margarine, cooking fat and cheese free from rationing.

June 1954 - meat no longer rationed. Ration books were now no longer required.

1946

During this year there were fears of a world famine and, for the first time, bread was rationed in Britain. Oatmeal had been a very important food during the whole of the war period; now, with a shortage of bread, it was used even more.

Rice was no longer imported; quantities of cereals for animal feed were reduced. The hopes for increased rations of meat, bacon and eggs were not realised.

The government did make this year, however, a special increase of 1½ lb (675 g) sugar on each ration book to allow for Christmas cooking. Sweeter cakes and puddings and even sweetmeats could be made.

1947 TO 1949

The meat ration was reduced from 1s 2d (6p) to 1s 0d (5p). Canned meat and unrationed offal, like tripe, were eagerly bought.

Although the rations were severe, many foods that had not been brought into this country before were beginning to appear. I well remember Brazil nuts being obtainable for Christmas 1947. More unusual vegetables, such as red and green peppers, were also coming into the shops.

The official Ministry information shows no special increases of any foods for Christmas that year but there was extra sugar for jam-making over a four-week period during the summer. Bread and preserves were de-rationed in 1948.

There were sparse supplies of oranges, from which people could make real marmalade, rather than one based upon apples and carrots, as in the past.

BBC Television had been resumed. I did the cooking in the first BBC Women's magazine programme in November 1947 and continued doing this throughout the fifties and early sixties.

FOOD FACTS

On 24 April 1947 the Home Secretary publically confirmed that there was still much valuable work being done by the WVS. Their soup recipe on page 104 is very appropriately named in view of the work they were doing then, and still do, to help the elderly. The service was honoured by the word Royal being added to its title by the Queen in 1966. So today it is the WRVS.

1950 TO 1954

During this period the various basic foods gradually became de-rationed, as I have noted above, and it was now much easier to plan meals, for so many other foods were appearing in the shops. There were better supplies of fish, vegetables, fruit and poultry.

In 1952 I was able to demonstrate a fairly basic pre-

war Christmas Pudding and Cake on BBC TV. These recipes were repeated in 1953; then in 1954 I was able to show viewers the recipes I still use to this day: you will find them on pages 108-9.

Don't waste bread by letting it get stale

Much of my work on television during the early 1950s was on basic cooking, demonstrating how to cook interesting fish and vegetable dishes and, when meat came off the ration, choose the correct cuts of meat and appetising dishes using these. There was great interest in baking. When rationing ended it seemed that everyone wanted to make perfect cakes, particularly Victoria Sandwiches.

THE MINISTRY OF FOOD

It was still very important for the Ministry to control foods and to give help to people. The Food Advisers still continued their work, appearing at Agricultural Shows and other venues and also giving demonstrations to young women leaving the services, who were now cooking for the first time.

Suffolk Rusks

Preparation time: 10 minutes

Cooking time: 18-20 minutes

Quantity: Makes 24 rusks

8 oz (225 g) self-raising flour or plain flour sifted with 2 teaspoons baking powder
pinch salt
1½ oz (40 g) margarine
1 tablespoon caster sugar, optional
¼ pint (150 ml) milk

Preheat the oven to 200°C (400°F), Gas Mark 6. Sift the flour, or flour and baking powder, and salt, rub in the margarine, add the sugar. Blend with enough milk to make a soft rolling consistency. Roll out to ¾ inch (2 cm) in thickness. Cut into 12 rounds. Put on an ungreased baking tray; bake for 8 minutes, or until firm enough to handle. Remove from the oven, lower the heat to 180°C (350*°F), Gas Mark 4. Cut each round in half horizontally. Place the cut side downwards on to baking trays. Bake for 10 minutes, or until golden brown and crisp.

Variation: do make these with butter when possible.

Cobs

Preparation time: 5-6 minutes

Cooking time: 10 minutes

Quantity: 10-12 helpings

These are an excellent substitute for bread. They are made in minutes and must be eaten fresh. They freeze well.

8 oz (225 g) self-raising four or plain flour sifted with 2 teaspoons baking powder
pinch salt
1 oz (25 g) margarine
approximately ¼ pint (150 ml) milk

Preheat the oven to 230°C (450°F), Gas Mark 8. Lightly grease a baking tray. Sift the flour, or flour and baking powder, and salt into a bowl. Rub in the margarine. Add enough milk to make a soft binding consistency - the mixture must not be too stiff, but rather sticky. Divide the dough into 10-12 portions and roll into balls with floured hands. Place on the baking tray and cook for 10 minutes, or until they feel firm, are golden brown in colour and crisp. Eat the cobs when freshly baked.

Variation: like the Suffolk Rusks, these are excellent when made with butter instead of margarine.

OATMEAL

I have taken the following information from a special Ministry of Food leaflet of the period.

'Oatmeal is such an important food that the Government has undertaken to subsidise it. There are plentiful supplies of oatmeal and rolled oats at a price which is within reach of all.

'Scotland gives us oatmeal, the most valuable of our cereals, more nourishing even than wholemeal flour. Oatmeal is one of the simple foods on which our forefathers lived and throve. The cakes that King Alfred burned were, in all probability, oaten cakes and, for many a century, oatmeal played an important part in the countryman's daily diet. During the last hundred years other cereals have tended to oust it from the Englishman's table but today it is coming into its own once again.

'Why is oatmeal valuable? Because it not only builds our bodies and gives us energy but also helps to protect us from illness. Oatmeal contains even more of that elusive Vitamin B1 than wholemeal bread and far and away more than white flour. That is one reason why it is a "protective food". Another is that it gives us the elements that make bone and blood.'

Oatmeal for thickening soups and stews

To 2 pints (1.2 litres) of soup or stew add 1½-2 oz (40-50 g) oats. Fine, medium or coarse oatmeal should be added about 30 minutes before the end of the cooking time, but rolled oats need be added only 10 minutes before the end. Stir well to blend then simmer steadily after adding the oats. Stir from time to time to prevent the mixture sticking.

Oatmeal instead of nuts

Toast oatmeal or rolled oats on a tray in an oven preheated to 180°C (350°F), Gas Mark 4 for about 15 minutes or under a preheated grill for 6-8 minutes, or until golden in colour. This makes it tasty and digestible to sprinkle over fruit and individual sweets instead of chopped nuts.

Oatmeal Scones or Farls

PREPARATION TIME: 15 MINUTES

COOKING TIME: 12-15 MINUTES OR 10 MINUTES

QUANTITY: 12 SCONES

These scones, or farls, can be cooked in the oven or on a griddle (a bakestone). They are equally good as a savoury or sweet scone. The extra baking powder used is to compensate for the weight of oats.

8 oz (225 g) rolled oats or medium oatmeal
2 oz (50 g) self-raising flour sifted with 1 teaspoon baking powder or plain flour sifted with 1½ teaspoons baking powder
good pinch salt
1-1½ oz (25-40 g) margarine or cooking fat
1-2 oz (25-50 g) sugar for sweet scones
approximately ¼ pint (150 ml) milk

Put the oats into a mixing bowl, sift the flour, baking powder and salt into the bowl. Rub in the margarine or fat, add the sugar, if using this, and enough milk to make a fairly firm rolling consistency.

Roll out the dough on a board coated with a little flour until approximately ½ inch (1 cm) thick, if baking the scones, but slightly less than that if cooking on the griddle. Cut into small rounds or triangles.

If baking the scones: preheat the oven to 220°C (450°F), Gas Mark 7. Lightly grease a baking tray. Add the scones and bake for 12-15 minutes.

If cooking on a griddle: grease then preheat the griddle. To test if this is the right heat shake on a little flour, it should turn golden in colour within 1 minute but no shorter a time.

Put the scones on the griddle, cook steadily for 5 minutes, turn over and cook for the same time on the second side.

Lift the scones on to a clean teacloth, placed on a wire cooling tray, and cover with the cloth. This keeps the scones pleasantly moist.

Variations: To give an attractive appearance to the scones brush the tops with a little milk and sprinkle with a small amount of rolled oats before baking. This is not suitable when cooking the scones on the griddle.

Cheese Scones: these are very good for a packed meal. Use just 1 oz (25 g) margarine or cooking fat and add 2 oz (50 g) or even 3 oz (75 g) grated cheese, if you can spare it. Sift a little pepper and dry mustard powder with the flour and baking powder as well as the salt.

Fruit Scones:if you have any dried fruit to spare add about 2 oz (50 g) to the flour mixture.

Oatmeal Treacle Scones: omit the sugar and add 1-2 tablespoons black treacle. You will need a little less milk.

RECIPES FROM FOOD FIRMS

As well as the Ministry of Food, many food firms also supplied recipes for the public. The following recipes were given by Omo, Batchelors and Stork. They are not quite as originally printed, for I have inserted the metric measures, preparation time, etc. The quantities of ingredients and method are as the original recipes.

Local authorities also helped to give people imaginative ideas for their meals .

Potato and Cheese Fritters

Preparation time: 15 minutes

Cooking time: 5-6 minutes

Quantity: 4 helpings

For the batter:

3 oz (75 g) plain flour

1 teaspoon baking powder

¼ pint (150 ml) milk and water

2 Oxo cubes or 1 heaped teaspoon fluid Oxo

little Worcestershire sauce

2 oz (50 g) cheese, grated

salt and pepper

3 large cooked potatoes, new potatoes are ideal, if small use 6, sliced

For frying:

little cooking fat or dripping

Blend the flour, baking powder and milk and water to make a smooth batter. Add the Oxo, Worcestershire sauce, half the cheese and a little seasoning.

Dip the sliced potatoes into the batter. Heat the fat or dripping and drop the potato slices into the hot fat. Fry them on both sides until golden. Sprinkle with the remaining grated cheese and serve hot.

Cheese and Lentil Pie

Preparation time: 30 minutes

Cooking time: 50 minutes

Quantity: 4 helpings

8 oz (225 g) lentils

½ tablespoon chopped onion, leek or chives

2 Oxo cubes or 1 heaped teaspoon fluid Oxo

½ pint (300 ml) water

salt and pepper

6 oz (175 g) cheese, grated

1 lb (450 g) mashed potatoes

little dripping

Soak the lentils overnight in cold water to cover. Drain then put them into a pan with the onion, leek or chives, the Oxo cubes or fluid Oxo and the ½ pint (300 ml) water. Cover the pan tightly and cook until the lentils are fairly dry. Season and mix with the cheese.

Preheat the oven to 200°C (400°F), Gas Mark 6. Spoon the lentil mixture into a 2 pint (1.2 litre) greased dish. Top with the mashed potatoes. Add the dripping in small pieces and bake for 20 minutes.

Variation: Use haricot beans instead of lentils. As these take longer to tenderize, you should increase the amount of water to 1 pint (600 ml).

Green Pea Torte

QUANTITY: FOR 3 OR 4 PEOPLE

Make pastry using 2½-3 oz (65-75 g) flour, rub in 1½ oz (40 g) fat, mix with a very little milk or water. Roll very thinly in a strip.

Place on a greased baking tin or sheet and bake for 10 minutes in a quick oven, 200°C (400°F), Gas Mark 6. Meanwhile, heat a tin of Batchelors Peas.

Lift the cooked pastry from the baking sheet on to a hot dish. Cover the pastry with hot peas, sprinkle with grated cheese, place under the grill for 1 minute and serve at once.

Old Folks Soup

PREPARATION TIME: 30 MINUTES

COOKING TIME: 40 MINUTES

QUANTITY: 4-5 HELPINGS

The work of the WVS may have changed somewhat since wartime and the period immediately after the war, but they continue to give wonderful help to people, including the old and less fit. This is typical of the kind of satisfying meal in a soup they offer to old folks, perhaps in a Meals on Wheels lunch.

1 oz (25 g) dripping or cooking fat
2 oz (50 g) carrots, sliced
2 oz (50 g) turnips, diced
1 medium onion, finely chopped
1 leek, thinly sliced
1 small celery stick, finely chopped
1½ oz (40 g) flour
2 pints (1.2 litres) stock
salt and pepper
6 oz (175 g) sausages or sausagemeat

Melt the dripping or cooking fat in a saucepan, add the vegetables and fry gently for a few minutes. Add the flour and blend with the vegetables, then pour in the stock. Stir briskly as the liquid comes to the boil and the soup thickens. Season to taste.

Cook until the vegetables are nearly tender. Meanwhile, skin the sausages, if using, and form the meat into small balls with floured fingers. Drop into the soup and simmer for 15 minutes.

Piquant Tripe

Wash 1 lb (450 g) dressed tripe in cold water then put into a saucepan with sufficient fresh water to cover, a bay leaf and a little seasoning. Cover the pan, bring to the boil and simmer gently for 1½ hours.

Remove the tripe from the pan, cut into small pieces. Save ½ pint (300 ml) of the liquid.

Heat 1½ oz (40 g) margarine in a pan, stir in 2 oz (50 g) flour, add the tripe liquid and ½ pint (300 ml) milk. Stir constantly as the sauce comes to the boil and thickens.

Add the tripe and heat, then add 3 tablespoons chopped gherkins and 2 teaspoons mustard blended with 1 tablespoon vinegar. Heat gently, being careful not to let the sauce boil, before serving the tripe.

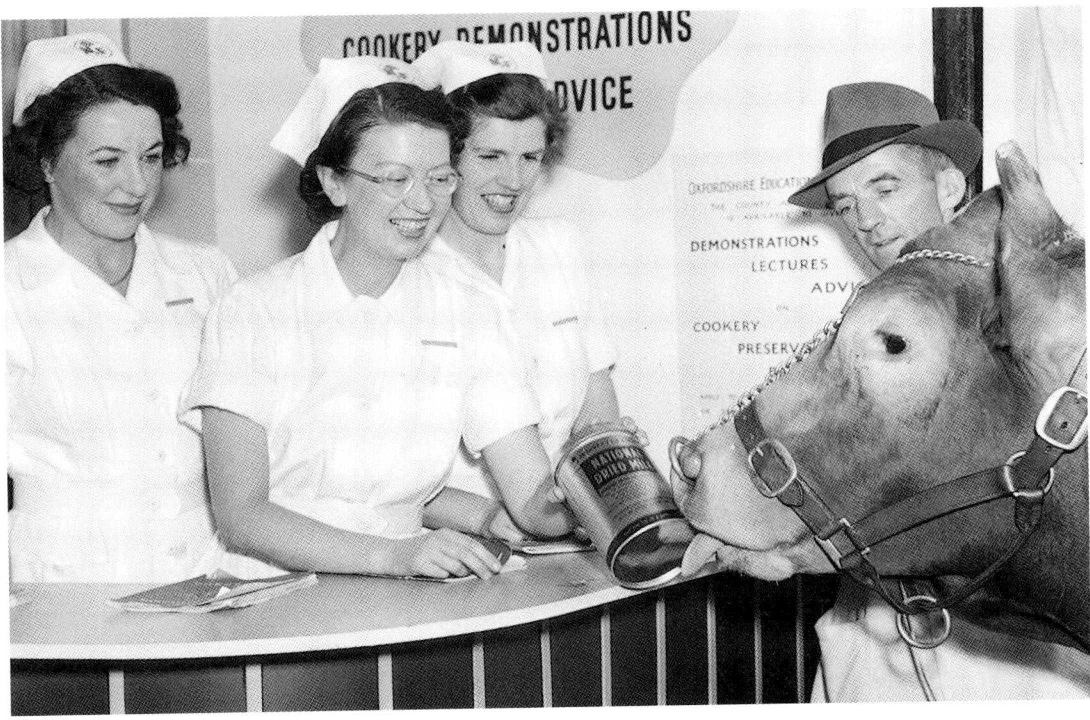

Stuffed Pigeons

In the early 1950s when grain was so very precious there was a plague of pigeons, who were eating it.

Farmers asked me to demonstrate pigeon dishes to persuade the public to make use of this very edible but, at the time, tiresome bird.

Halve young pigeons lengthways; remove as many bones as possible; spread sausagemeat against the cut side, then coat in beaten egg and crisp breadcrumbs.

Fry in hot fat until crisp and brown all over; lower the heat and continue cooking for 10-15 minutes. Serve with creamed potatoes and a green vegetable.

RETURN OF FRUIT

The return of oranges, lemons and other citrus fruits and bananas was one of the most exciting things, for these made such a difference to our lifestyle.

Before fresh bananas became available dried bananas were on sale. These were dark brown, rather chewy in texture and sweet. They were very pleasant if sliced and cooked in a little lemon-flavoured sugar syrup or chopped and added to a steamed pudding mixture with other dried fruit. Many people ate them as a snack.

Two recipes that follow make use of citrus fruit.

Banana Cream

PREPARATION TIME: 10 MINUTES

NO COOKING IF CUSTARD MADE

QUANTITY: 4 HELPINGS

This was a delicious dessert that became possible when bananas came back

3 large ripe bananas
2 tablespoons cold water
½ oz (15 g) gelatine*
¼ pint (150 ml) custard (page 38)
½ pint (300 ml) evaporated milk, whipped (page 39)
sugar, to taste
*** this would be one sachet of today's gelatine**

Mash the bananas until a pulp. Pour the water into a basin, add the gelatine and allow to stand for 2 minutes then dissolve over hot, but not boiling, water. Add to the warm custard with the bananas, blend together.

Leave in a cool place until the mixture begins to stiffen then fold in the whipped evaporated milk with sugar to taste.

Spoon into glasses and chill well.

Canary Pudding

PREPARATION TIME: 20 MINUTES

COOKING TIME: 1½ HOURS

QUANTITY: 4 HELPINGS

3 oz (75 g) margarine
4 oz (100 g) caster sugar
2 teaspoons finely grated lemon rind
2 reconstituted dried or fresh eggs
4 oz (100 g) self-raising flour or plain flour sifted with 1 teaspoon baking powder
2 tablespoons lemon juice

Cream the margarine, sugar and lemon rind until soft and light. Beat the eggs lightly and add gradually to the creamed mixture. Sift the flour, or flour and baking powder, and add to the other ingredients with the lemon juice.

Grease a 1½ pint (900 ml) basin, put in the mixture, cover with greased greaseproof paper and steam over boiling water for 45 minutes then lower the heat and steam more gently for a further 45 minutes.

Serve with Lemon Sauce (see below).

Lemon Sauce

Put 2 oz (50 g) sugar and ¼ pint (150 ml) water into a small saucepan with 2 teaspoons very finely grated lemon zest.

Stir over a low heat until the sugar dissolves.

Blend 1 teaspoon cornflour with 2 tablespoons lemon juice. Add to the ingredients in the saucepan and stir over a low heat until the sauce thickens and becomes clear.

Cheese and Haddock Soufflé

PREPARATION TIME: 15 MINUTES

COOKING TIME: 30-35 MINUTES

QUANTITY: 4 HELPINGS

As fresh eggs became more plentiful, eventually being de-restricted in March 1953, many enthusiastic cooks turned their attention to making soufflés, for they felt that this was the dish for which fresh eggs were essential. Although the result is certainly better with shell eggs, soufflés can be made with dried eggs very happily. Cream, which had been unavailable right through the years of rationing, became available again from April 1953 - just in time for the Queen's Coronation!.

1 oz (25 g) butter or margarine
1 oz (25 g) flour
¼ pint (150 ml) milk
3 tablespoons extra milk or cream
3 eggs
1 egg white
4 oz (100 g) mature Cheddar cheese, grated
4 oz (100 g) cooked smoked haddock, finely flaked
salt and pepper

Preheat the oven to 190°C (375°F), Gas Mark 5. Grease a 6-7 inch (15-18 cm) soufflé dish.

Heat the butter or margarine in a saucepan, stir in the flour, then add the milk and cream, if using this. Whisk hard as the sauce comes to the boil and thickens. Remove from the heat.

Separate the eggs. Add the egg yolks to the sauce, put the whites with the extra egg white. Blend the cheese and fish with the other ingredients in the saucepan. Add seasoning to taste. Whisk the whites

until they stand in soft peaks, and fold carefully into the cheese and fish mixture.

Spoon into the soufflé dish and bake in the preheated oven for 30-35 minutes, or until well risen and golden brown. Serve at once.

Variation: This soufflé can be made with dried eggs. Reconstitute 3 or 4 eggs in the usual way and add to the sauce in exactly the same way as fresh eggs. You have no whites to whisk separately. The soufflé will rise well, but will not be quite as light as when fresh eggs are chosen.

Victoria Sandwich

PREPARATION TIME: 25 MINUTES

COOKING TIME: 20 MINUTES

QUANTITY: MAKES 1 SPONGE CAKE

Most cooks wanted to achieve a perfect Victoria Sandwich and, in the 1950s at various fêtes and shows, there were countless competitions for this sponge cake. The old-fashioned method of using the eggs instead of weights was still used; this made absolutely certain the fat, sugar and flour exactly matched the weight of the eggs (in their shells).

6 oz (175 g) butter or margarine
6 oz (175 g) caster sugar
3 eggs - size 1 or 2
6 oz (175 g) self-raising flour or plain flour sifted with 2 teaspoons baking powder
For the filling and topping:
jam
caster sugar

Preheat the oven to 180-190°C (350-375°F), Gas Mark 4-5. Ovens vary appreciably and it is wise to use the lower setting the first time you make this sponge cake. Grease and flour or line two 7½-8 inch (19-20 cm)

round sandwich tins.

Cream the butter or margarine and sugar until soft and light. Whisk the eggs and gradually beat into the creamed mixture, adding a little of the flour if the mixture looks like curdling. Sift the flour, or flour and baking powder, and fold into the other ingredients.

Spoon into the tins and bake side by side in the preheated oven for approximately 20 minutes or until firm to the touch. Cool in the tins for a few minutes then invert on to a folded teacloth on the palm of your hand then invert on to a wire cooling rack. This ensures that the top of the delicate cake is not marked by the tray.

When cold, sandwich together with jam and top with a sprinkling of caster sugar.

Christmas Cake of 1954

PREPARATION TIME: 35 MINUTES

COOKING TIME: SEE METHOD

QUANTITY: MAKES 1 CAKE

This is the cake that has won so much praise over the years from people who make it. Ovens vary a great deal and this is particularly obvious when baking rich fruit cakes, such as this one, so test carefully and check baking as indicated in the method.

12 oz (350 g) plain flour
1 teaspoon ground cinnamon
1 teaspoon mixed spice
4 oz (110 g*) candied peel, chopped
2 lb (900 g) mixed dried fruit, preferably 1 lb (450 g) currants, 8 oz (225 g) sultanas, 8 oz (225 g) seedless raisins
2-4 oz (50-110 g*) blanched almonds, chopped
4 oz (110 g*) glacé cherries, chopped
4 large eggs
4 tablespoons milk, sherry, brandy or rum
finely grated rind 1 lemon
finely grated rind 1 orange (optional)
8 oz (225 g) butter or margarine
8 oz (225 g) sugar, preferably dark moist brown sugar
1 tablespoon black treacle or golden syrup
*** use this metrication**

Preparing the tin: this is a rich Christmas cake that should ideally be made at least one month before Christmas. It gives the right amount of ingredients for a 9 inch (23 cm) round or 8 inch (20 cm) square cake. Prepare the tin carefully. Line the bottom of the tin with a double round of brown paper and cover this with a double thickness of lightly greased greaseproof paper. Line the sides of the tin with greased greaseproof paper. Tie a deep band of brown paper around the outside of the tin.

Preparing the cake: sift together all the dry ingredients. Mix together the peel, fruit, almonds and cherries (if these are slightly sticky then mix with a little of the flour). Blend the eggs with the milk, sherry, brandy or rum. Cream together the lemon and orange rinds with the butter or margarine, sugar and treacle or golden syrup until soft. Do not over-beat: this cake does not need much beating. Gradually blend in the egg mixture and sifted dry ingredients. Stir in all the fruit. Put the mixture into the tin, smooth flat on top, then press with damp knuckles to help keep the cake moist on top.

Bake in the centre of a moderate oven, 160°C (325°F), Gas Mark 3 for about 1½ hours then lower the oven to cool 140-150°C (275-300°F), Gas Mark 1-2 for

about another 2 hours. Baking times for rich fruit cakes like this vary considerably according to the particular oven, so test it carefully.

To test rich fruit cakes: After the first third of the cooking time the cake should still be very pale in colour. If darkening too much, lower the oven temperature rather sooner than indicated above. Test again at the end of the second third of the cooking time. The cake should still be fairly soft on top but a good golden colour;, if becoming too dark then lower the heat still further. To test if completely cooked at the end of the cooking time, check that the cake has shrunk away from the sides of the tin then listen very carefully. An uncooked rich fruit cake makes a distinct humming noise. When completely cooked it is absolutely silent.

Variation: Add 4 oz (110 g - use this metrication) finely diced uncooked apricots and 2 oz (50 g) ground almonds to the above mixture.*

Christmas Pudding of 1954

Preparation time: 40 minutes

Cooking time: 6-8 hours then 2-3 hours

Quantity: 10-12 helpings

4 oz (110 g*) fine soft breadcrumbs
2 oz (50 g) flour, preferably plain
4 oz (110 g*) shredded suet
4 oz (110 g*) moist brown sugar
8 oz (225 g) seedless or stoned and chopped raisins
4 oz (110 g*) sultanas
4 oz (110 g*) currants
2 oz (50 g) dried apricots, finely chopped
1 oz (25 g) dried prunes, stoned and finely chopped
4 oz (110 g*) mixed candied peel, chopped
2 oz (50 g) glacé cherries, chopped
2 oz (50 g) cooking apple (weight when peeled), grated
2 oz (50 g) carrots (weight when peeled), grated
2 oz (50 g) blanched almonds, chopped
½ teaspoon grated lemon rind
½ teaspoon grated orange rind
¼-½ teaspoon ground nutmeg
½-1 teaspoon mixed spice
¼-½ teaspoon ground cinnamon
2 large eggs
1½ teaspoons lemon juice
1½ teaspoons orange juice
1½ teaspoons black treacle
4 tablespoons stout or ale
½ wineglass brandy or rum
*** use this metrication**

Mix all the ingredients together. I like to leave the uncooked pudding mixture standing overnight, so that the flavours blend better. It also allows all members of the family to stir the mixture and wish.

Grease two 2½ pint (1.5 litre) or one 4½ pint (2.5 litre) basins; put in the mixture. Cover well with greased greaseproof paper and foil. A Christmas Pudding does not rise in the same way as a light sponge pudding but it swells in cooking so never fill the basin too full. If you press the mixture down firmly you can cut neater slices of the cooked pudding, but my recipe gives a crumbly pudding rather than a solid one.

Steam each pudding for 6-8 hours depending upon the size; take off the damp covers at once; cool the puddings, then put on dry covers. Store the pudding in a cool dry place.

On Christmas Day, steam the pudding for another 2-3 hours before serving.

INDEX

ACKNOWLEDGEMENTS

I should like to express my gratitude to the many people who passed on their carefully preserved mementos of the days leading up to the VE and VJ Days in 1945 and especially to the following people and organizations.

My friends who were in the Ministry of Food Advice Division and who lent me leaflets and pictures: Mary Bass, Gwen Conacher, Joan Peters, and also Georgie Pender for her help in providing information about the Tube Refreshment Service.

Margaret Coombes, Jane Hutchinson, Edna Taylor and McDougalls, who lent me cherished cookery books.

The Ministry of Agriculture, Fisheries and Food (MAFF) for the wartime food information leaflets and the records they sent me about food rationing.

The Department of Education for a wartime leaflet and recipes on canteen meals for school children.

The Savoy Group of Hotels and the Dorchester Hotel for their menus.

The Unilever archive for food leaflets and recipes.

The Press Departments of Buckingham Palace, The Guildhall and 10 Downing Street, who searched through their records to see what events took place in 1945.

The WRVS and especially their archivist, Mrs Megan Keable, for the loan of material from their archive, including wartime recipe booklets and a 'History of the WRVS'.

The various embassies and government offices I contacted to learn about Victory Day memories in other countries.

My sister Elizabeth Brown-Moen for the picture and information about Norwegian celebrations.

Marguerite Patten

Picture Credits

Many of the photographs in this book are unidentified, having been taken on or around VE and VJ Days in Britain. Where more details are known they have been included in the following list.

Aftenpostens/Jugald Mollerstad 87 (VE Day in Oslo, Norway)

Caledonian Newspapers Ltd 68 top (cheering VE Day on the Glasgow buses); 107 (VJ Day shopping queue in Glasgow)

Faber and Faber/Joy Batchelor (from *Food Without Fuss* by Josephine Terry) 18

Harrods Archive 68 bottom

Hulton Deutsch Front Cover top and bottom; Back Cover centre; 3; 9; 12-13 (an American serviceman joins a celebration lunch in England); 22; 37; 40-1; 46 (VE Day children's street party in Clapham, London); 50-51 (WVS mobile canteen 'somewhere in England'); 58; 62-63; 67 (teabreak in unidentified aircraft factory); 70 bottom right; 73; 74-75; 76 (after the VE Day service, St Paul's Cathedral, London); 77; 79 (New Zealand troops march through London); 82 (Canadian servicemen join celebrations in the street); 88-89; 98-99 (the day sweet rationing ended in 1953)

Edith Hurst 32-33 (VE Day street party in Ipswich)

Imperial War Museum 103

Robert Opie Back Cover top left, top right, bottom left and bottom right; 4 top left; 19; 39; 45; 55; 64; 84; 90

Range Pictures Ltd 4-5; 81 (New York celebrates the end of war in Europe)

Savoy Group Press Office 70 top and bottom left